"A grandmother is a little bit parent,

a little bit teacher, and a little bit best friend."

Author Unknown

From Grandma to you

Childcare Wisdom for a New Generation

Joan D. Hellstrom, Susan D. Findlay, Connie E. Ray

Dr. Homer R. Rich

2nd Edition

Ogden Litho, Inc., P.O. Box 6, Ogden, UT 84405
Phone: (801) 399-5546 Fax: (801) 621-4609
Email: art@ogdenlitho.com
Web: www.ogdenlitho.com

Library of Congress Cataloging-in-Publication Data
From Grandma to You: Childcare Wisdom for a New Generation / [edited by] Joan
Hellstrom, Susan Findlay, Connie Ray.
   p. cm.
  Includes index.
  ISBN 978-1-5323-3886-1
  Second Edition
1. Grandmothers. 2. Grandparent and Child. 3. I. Hellstrom, Joan. II. Findlay, Susan. III.
Ray, Connie (Connie E.)

First Edition, 2005
Second Edition, 2017

10 9 8 7 6 5 4 3 2 1
Published by Ogden Litho, Inc.
© 2017 Joan Hellstrom, Susan Findlay, Connie Ray
Printed and bound in the U.S.A.

Before following any advice or practice suggestions in this book, it is recommended that you consult your doctor as to its suitability. The publishers and the authors cannot accept any responsibility for any injuries or damage incurred as a result of following the advice in this book, or of using any of the therapeutic techniques described or mentioned here.

CONTENTS

EPIGRAPH
The Legacy

by Alice Redd Rich, 1879-1968

To you grandchildren, I would leave today

some footprint, etched in honest clarity;

a dream that questing hearts may find in me

some lasting guideposts toward a better way.

As grasses drink the silver dews and rains,

so you, the petaled bloom of love, may know

the strength and love the passing years bestow,

the heartbeats that my faith in you ordains.

May it be said, when I am gone, "Her ways

were gentle and her hopeful homely wit

gave her an understanding heart to fit

the common path she walked for happier days."

As essence of her life—her legacy—

will always walk with us in memory.

DEDICATION

In memory of Fredonna Strickler Dixon–oma, mother, teacher, and friend.

FOREWORD

The cycle of mothering turns on greased gears. Most of us don't know exactly when we first experienced the stirring of the force that would eventually influence every aspect of our lives. The maternal instinct is tricky that way–subtle, conniving, and infinitely patient, until one day the initial mothering phase unceremoniously stops. What follows is an interlude of uncertainty, when tried-and-true techniques just don't seem to work anymore. However, if you're lucky, the cycle bursts to life again and the most thrilling, rewarding, and timeless phase begins–grandmothering!

Noted anthropologist Margaret Mead knew the benefits of the final phase of mothering. In Blackberry Winter, she wrote, "Everyone needs to have access both to grandparents and grandchildren in order to be a full human being." We believe there are few treasures that can compare to the mothering moments that have touched generations of hearts and souls. They connect us in so many ways–mother to daughter, grandmother to grandchild, friend to friend, and every other imaginable mutually caring relationship.

As grandmothers, ourselves, we share with you these bits of tradition and wisdom that have defined many families. They are gems of inheritance that make us realize how enduring are the tried-and-true advice, remedies, and hints. Along with the counsel of over sixty grandmothers, a well-loved and trusted pediatrician shares child-care methods and suggestions from his fifty-one-year practice. These recommendations have benefited hundreds of grandmothers, mothers, and daughters. Enjoy!

PREFACE

Parenting is the grandest adventure of all, I've been told. Parenting is also risky. Still, it saddens me when parents fail to enjoy the ride; they miss out on all the joys that parenting brings. Successful parenting requires total investment, involvement, courage, and faith; but the rewards outweigh the price. Now, grandparenting–that is definitely one of life's greatest adventures; however, I see more of the joy than the risk with my grandson Ben.

Ben's pouty baby lips make an exaggerated O as he says snow. My grandson is almost two, and everything is bright and beautiful to a two-year-old. I watch his eyes and wonder what is going on in his little mind. I look where he looks and try to imagine how it would be to see falling snow again for the first time. He tries to grab the flakes with his hands until I show him how to catch them on his tongue. He likes that. Can he perceive the muffled silence? I don't think so. As yet, he doesn't seem to care much for silence. We have other days like this, Ben and I. He communes with nature, and I eavesdrop.

I wasn't expecting the flood of emotion that accompanied his birth–part relief and gratitude, but also something else. We were connected, instantly linked by some eternal genetic chain. Amazed, I wondered, Why him? Why now? Had we made some pre-earthly pact? Or was it just kismet? With his birth, the torch was to pass to another generation. My own stint on that roller coaster of expectation and exhaustion called motherhood was behind me. My reward: time to do things for me, and I deserved it. Grandmothers are supposed to be detached, sensible advisors–I thought. Then Ben came with his own unique perspectives, and they didn't match with the prevailing logic.

The phenomenon that is Ben lives in a natural world governed by the wants and needs of his senses, and I am drawn into it. Urged on by the magnetism of his budding intelligence, I begin a practice advocated by Emerson–to look at the world with new eyes. The seasons don't just change; they explode with potential, waiting to be embraced. The grass seems greener, the rain gentler, the blossoms sweeter, and the friends dearer. As fresh views replace stale perspectives, I feel liberated from the analytical world and free to enjoy beauty for beauty's sake.

With me as Ben's accomplice, discovery possibilities are endless. At first, I decided where we would go and what we would investigate, but that state of affairs is long gone now. It ends with an eager tug on my arm and the words, "Grum, ride." I ask him where he wants to ride. "Dig-digs and dumps," he answers. It would take a stronger resolve than mine to resist his hopeful pleas. And so we're off to explore the world of loaders, dumpers, and scoops. His face registers pure unabashed joy when he spots earthmoving equipment of any character or color. In fact, he and I have become truck aficionados.

In his immediate surroundings, when he's under the power of his own stocky legs, Ben is a passionate observer. He does more than play in the dirt. He experiences dirt. He lays in it, buries his hands in it, tastes it, and throws it.

When he smells flowers, he thrusts his whole face into the petals; and when the autumn leaves are piled high, he dives in with abandon. Despite his almost inexhaustible energy, Ben will often concentrate very intensely. He will put something right up next to his eyes or bend close for a better view and then, with a furrowed brow, ponder whatever has caught his attention. To study crawly creatures, he throws himself down on his belly for a bug's-eye-view. Squatting on his haunches, he watches an earthworm as it stretches and contracts along a path through the soil. I show him how he can pick one up with a stick, but he's not interested in disturbing the worm from its environment. Thoreau couldn't have been more circumspect.

Yet most of all, Ben is happy; his countenance radiates with an irresistible inner light. Perhaps it is this ebullience that captivates me so—his great lust for life. Somehow, without realizing it, we lose the enthusiasm and passion for nature that we were born with—the fallen casualty of responsibilities, schedules, and deadlines. However, life is full of opportunities to get it back. Do what you can to regain a passion for nature—right here, right now. A spring snowstorm is my Walden; the baby in my arms, my looking glass; and nature herself, my tutor. In this quiet moment, life, as Emerson says, is reduced to its lowest terms. Ben is because of me and I am made better because of him. I carry him, but he leads me from one discovery to another. Like all of God's creations, he is a precious gift. I make a silent promise that I will cherish this moment in time as long as I can.

—Grandma Connie

PREFACE TO THE 2ND EDITION

While writing *From Grandma to You* we belived that "grandmothering" was the final phase of mothering. Well, fifteen years have flown by and the three of us now realize how short sighted we were. Believe it or not, we are quickly moving on to "great-grandmothering" and loving it!

Because the questions and concerns new mothers ask are the same year after year, we have been encouraged to reprint *From Grandma to You* and make the book available once again. We hope the simple stories and gentle advice in these pages will continue to be a source of comfort to mothers, grandmothers, and yes, even great-grandmothers!

"Life is a flame that is always burning itself out, but it catches fire again every time a child is born." - George Bernard Shaw

With love,

Joan, Susan, and Connie

INTRODUCTION
A Word about Dr. Homer R. Rich

In addition to the sage advice of grandmothers, we have included suggestions and anecdotes from a highly respected, longtime pediatrician, Dr. Rich.

Dr. Rich's office was unique—a tiny, antiquated inner-city office, absent of computers, fax machines, and other modern technology. Dr. Rich believed that mothers made an appointment with the doctor, not an assistant. If blood pressure or temperature were to be taken, Dr. Rich did it himself, and he gave all shots himself. Over the course of his fifty-one years of practice, Dr. Rich was more than a pediatrician for his patients. He was also their counselor and friend. Three generations of patients grew up under his care, and they speak about him with praise, gratitude, and love.

Dr. Rich retired from medical practice in 1999, just shy of his 83rd birthday. Not just a physician, he was also a healer of the body and spirit. He was also the father of six children, 22 grandchildren, 96 great-grandchildren and 16 great-great-grandchildren. Here are some of the things Dr. Rich's former patients had to say about him:

Dr. Rich's Moms Say:

I will never forget the time Dr. Rich looked at me and said, "Can you understand what I am saying?" I replied, "Oh, yes, I am a speech pathologist. I have worked with lots of children with speech problems!"

- Dr. Rich was the "fastest needle in the West!"

- Dr. Rich always told me that mothers were the best detectives.

- My early remedy for diaper rash—scorching flour in the oven and applying it to the baby's bottom like powder. When taking my baby to Dr. Rich for a monthly examination, he removed her diaper and exclaimed, "Gee, that smells just like the gravy my mother used to make!"

- Dr. Rich always reassured me by saying, "Don't worry about anything. Leave all of your worries to me."

- Dr. Rich taught us to not discourage our child's independence. He said, "You can't raise your child in a glass cage."

- Dr. Rich's advice for thumb-sucking was, "If it makes you gag, turn your head. If it makes your neighbors gag, let them. Kids will quit sucking their thumbs when they get married."

- Dr. Rich's word superseded the then-famous Dr. Spock in the raising of our children.

- Do your children sleep in their own beds, and in their own rooms? Dr. Rich knew that moms and dads need time for themselves, too.

- For a bee sting, Dr. Rich recommended putting my child's hand in mud and pouring myself a drink!

- Dr. Rich listened to mothers. I will never forget the time he said to me, "If you are concerned, I am concerned," then went on to say that mothers know their children better than anyone else and should be listened to.

- Dr. Rich taught us how and when to hold loved ones close and how and when to let them go. All in all, what a nice gift we can now pass on as grandparents.

A Word from Dr. Rich

My love for pediatric medicine was formed as a young intern while rotating through the various medical specialties at the old Salt Lake County Hospital over fifty years ago. On the pediatric service, I discovered I was working with the very finest folks–young mothers and their children. The work was rewarding and I was happy there. So, although pediatrics is one of the worst-paying medical specialty fields, I made a choice early on that I would pursue what I loved and live life as a happy man no matter what the pay scale was.

At the height of my business, I had three rooms and they were always full. But I wanted to be sure my mothers knew I was willing to spend as much time with them as they needed because no one likes to be hurried–especially not a new mother. First, I'd sit with a new mother and baby, and we'd talk about her problems and concerns. I'd examine the baby carefully; then type my report so each mother went home with written instructions she could refer to later. I was a terrible typist, but I knew some mothers had a hard time understanding me and my handwriting wasn't very clear. In return, the first thousand mothers I assisted taught me most everything I knew about babies.

What a doctor learns in medical school constitutes only a fraction of what he will need in his practice. Every child is different, and no one rule works for everybody every time. Instead, a pediatrician's wisdom comes from years of practice, listening, and common sense, too! And that's where a grandmother's wisdom comes in–years and years of caring for children, of noticing what works and what doesn't, of seeing the "big picture," for making a child happy and healthy.

This book offers a dose of the legacy grandmothers have to leave us. As you read through this book, I hope you'll collect advice from the grandmothers surrounding you in your own life, as well as medical advice from your own physicians. Write it down so the next generation will have it. After all, one day this will be the legacy you leave the next generation of children.

—Homer Redd Rich, M.D.

CHAPTER ONE
Enjoying the Legacy of Motherhood
"Nothing is quite as good as experience."
—Homer Rich, M.D.

I wanted twelve children, but was blessed with seven. I loved motherhood; I get warm inside just thinking about those wonderful, trying, tired days. Every day I insisted on a quiet time for my children and myself. Although the kids often resisted quiet time, they usually fell right to sleep. I used the time to gather my thoughts and regroup for the rest of the day. **If you organize your routine to include time to recharge, you and your children will enjoy the benefits.**

My energetic, nine-month old grandson pulled himself up with anything and everything within his reach. Once, he tried to pull himself up with a floor lamp and sent it crashing right into his mother's head. Startled and angry, she grabbed my grandson and put him wailing into his crib, which made her feel guilty. I wanted to help her see this incident from a broader perspective. The lamp could be replaced easily, but the learning experience, for both her and my grandson, could have far-reaching effects. **Before becoming angry, pause long enough to consider such situations with patience and understanding–time-outs for mothers can be as important as time-outs for children.**

My grandma, a mother of fourteen, knew the baby blues were real, but she never had time to give in to them. She said there were nights she lacked the energy to even take her clothes off before she went to bed. I hope husbands and other care givers never let a new mom become that exhausted. **Whether nurturing her first, second, or tenth baby, all new mothers need love and assurance from those around her.** Step in with all the sensitive support and encouragement you can offer. I worry as my daughter juggles her career, family, and home. I often felt tense and conflicted when I was a young mother, and I can see that she does too. Moms of all generations have tiring schedules, emotional battles and exhausting physical demands placed upon them. Every woman's challenges differ, but to say that one is worse than another is as impossible as comparing apples and oranges.

My mother often said, **"A good night's rest cures most things."** She also recommended letting a few things go for another day in order to get a little more sleep at night.

By the time my third baby came along, I had learned to adjust my life to a baby's routine. I made the baby's feeding time to relax. I would go into my bedroom, put my feet up, lower the lights, and get away from everything while I nursed. **Don't struggle to make your baby's schedule fit your own—you'll end up frustrated and angry; instead, make the baby's schedule work for you.**

As a grandmother and teacher, my mother was a virtual child magnet. By just being her cheerful, optimistic self, she was a living reminder that **love and attention are what children crave.** I would often spot her sitting on the front porch with one of my children, encouraging them to listen to the birds, describing cloud formations, or looking at the beautiful flowers. She especially loved to describe the colors of a sunset filling the sky. No matter what the season or time of day, my mother could find something beautiful or amazing to talk to a child about.

Be thankful for the everyday chaos. It is sure lonely without it. You'll have plenty of time to think about that once your children are grown and gone from the house.

Next time you wonder if a high fever is too high or what to put on a bee sting, ask another mother, a grandmother, or a great-grandmother for advice. It will save you the time it would take you to research it and the trouble it would take to learn from trial-and-error. **Ask mothers, grandmothers, or great-grandmothers for their advice; they'll be happy to help.**

If you are an uptight mother, you probably have an uptight baby. Practice breathing deeply and remember to smile at your baby every time you look at him.

When my children were babies, I hung their diapers outside to dry. Sometimes a crisp, unexpected north wind would blow in, and I'd have to bring the diapers into the house, frozen stiff as boards, to finish drying. What a site that was! White flannel squares draped over every chair and table in the house. My enthusiasm for the day plummeted. There must be a more efficient way to accomplish this chore, I thought. It was my husband who discovered the perfect solution. During a visit to the hardware store, he found a small, folding, wooden dryer and brought it home to me. What a neat invention! As soon as my friends saw it, they wanted one too. I remember how excitedly we talked about those little racks. It's funny how such simple things impacted our lives. Today, automatic washers and dryers have made drying racks obsolete. **But remember, moms are still happy to find a little something to make their work easier, faster, or more economical.**

Keep life simple. My best advice is to abandon hard-and-fast schedules when they seem to make your life more complicated.

Use the time spent feeding your baby to do something you enjoy. Even in the middle of the night, as I fed my baby, I read—a pleasure I rarely had time to enjoy. Because of this, I never begrudged the time it took my babies to eat.

Naturally, finding the right husband was the major key. **A good dad makes being a good mom much easier and less stressful.**

One of the most special times in a mother's life is the little interval between your baby's birth and the resumption of the routine of everyday life. It should be a time to remember—a time filled with sunlight, rest, and soft woolly blankets, and the first exciting signs of the kind of person your baby will become. For this little space of time, you and your baby are the center of a small, protected universe. Only the things that concern the well-being of the two of you are really important, for the wise know when not to be wise, or cynical, or modern; and mothers have this wisdom. **They know that social upheavals and economic worries are flickers on the path; the things that bring love, health and laughter to children are the things that matter.** Hold on as long as you can to these fleeting moments.

When I was a first-time mom, I was so anxious for my baby to meet all the benchmarks of development that I often neglected to properly appreciate and delight in the experiences. I found myself wishing he could sit, or walk, or finally get that tooth. Remember, these firsts won't happen again. **Don't wish the miracles of childhood away—appreciate moments every day.**

Soon after our second child, Joey, was born, we bought some property in the country that bordered a dairy farm. Every weekend we escaped the city and took our youngsters to enjoy the peaceful rural atmosphere. One cool, sunny weekend, when Joey was six weeks old, his face was sunburned as we worked in the garden. His nose, cheek, and forehead blistered and peeled. People stopped me in the grocery store, or wherever I was, and asked me what was wrong with his face. I had to explain that I—his mother, the pediatrician—should have known better. Two weeks later, we returned to the country. To avoid a repeat sunburn, I placed Joey in his infant seat under a tree. My husband, daughter and I became engrossed with gardening, and since Joey was content, we didn't notice what was going on under the tree. Imagine our surprise when we saw eight huge dairy cows surrounding our baby! My instinct was to shout and wave hysterically while racing to save my baby, but I quickly realized this action might not be prudent, considering the size and number of the cows. Thank goodness the cows' mothering instincts were better than mine. They moved away gently and did not bother Joey. As a physician and a mother, I felt extremely guilty. But as my children became older and I became more experienced, I realized that every mother is faced with a long learning curve. **Learn to be patient with yourself—frustrating, difficult, or even scary experiences happen to everyone, including pediatricians.**

Being a far-away grandma makes me so sad; I just have to talk to my daughter every day on the phone. I also talk to my grandbaby every day. I call it cell phone bonding. Each morning my daughter puts the phone to the baby's ear so to hear my voice. I whisper sweet nothings to her, and she responds with precious little sounds, just as if I were holding her in my arms. What a thrill it is when I finally see her in person and she looks up at me with recognition. **Grandchildren need grandmothers, even if they live far apart.**

Parents of physically challenged children have many worries and concerns. But perhaps the greatest is, "Will my child be accepted and treated well by peers?" When my son had his left eye removed at twenty-two months, I decided I was going to let him be a boy, even though that meant allowing him to tumble and fall. Lack of depth perception and other visual and balance problems accompany the loss of an eye. So, when I took my toddler to the park, I let him climb the jungle gym, slides, and bars. He often fell, but eventually learned to compensate and maneuver himself through the playground. When he was older, he participated in team sports with the rest of his friends and grew to be quite a natural athlete. He has continued to enjoy many successes on and off the playing field. Sometimes you may have to hold your breath or look away to keep from crying, but allowing your child to take risks is giving that child the gift of acceptance. **I would encourage parents to allow their special youngster to explore and experience—and even fail—right along with their peers.**

Dr. Rich says:

I wish all mothers realized that babies are not fragile, but unusually durable. Every time a baby cries, it is not a disaster—bumps and bruises happen. Mothers, try to relax and enjoy your baby.

Baby blues, or postpartum depression, is a very real condition that can debilitate new mothers if not treated. Half of the women who suffer from postpartum depression have never been depressed before and find it difficult to understand what is happening to them and why. And simplistic advice from well-meaning friends and family members, such as working harder, is not only unhelpful, but insensitive. New mothers should be prepared to recognize the signs of postpartum depression without feeling shame or guilt. Postpartum depression can last up to one year and is both mentally and physically exhausting. Just having a little knowledge and a support system in place beforehand can be a tremendous help in dealing with the baby blues.

CHILD CARE HINTS TO REMEMBER

I remember mom saying

_____

_____

My own thoughts

_____

_____

CHAPTER TWO
It's Eatin' Time

"Mother, please pass the groceries."
—Homer Rich, M.D.

Our first child was born one month late and he came out fat and hungry. Even though I seemed to be producing enough milk, he wanted to nurse every two hours, day and night. After two weeks of almost constant nursing, I was exhausted and the baby still wasn't satisfied. Although experts caution against introducing solids to a baby's diet too early, fearing the development of food allergies, it just seemed to be common sense that my baby needed additional nourishment. So, with faith in my mothering instincts, I let him try rice cereal. Almost immediately he was happier, slept better and was more pleasant to be around. I continued to give him cereal supplements twice a day from then on. Of our four children, he was the only one that seemed to need anything other than mother's milk at such an early age. My experiences have taught me that it's important to be knowledgeable and well-advised, but with babies that's not always enough. **Sometimes you have to be pragmatic, trust your instincts, and do whatever works, within reason.**

I nursed three of my babies and bottle-fed two, and one is just as sweet, smart and healthy as the other. **Guilt is a choice—a feeling, and is totally worthless to either mother or child.**

After my first boy, I decided not to breast-feed my other children because I wanted the baby-in-the-house experience to be a family affair. My first son, followed by my other boys, learned to feed, diaper and take on lots of other tasks, depending on their abilities. One of the youngest guys thought it was his job to stand at the ready with a can of air freshener while I changed messy diapers. Although my children were all boys, they had baby dolls, bottles, and diapers. I felt they needed to learn to nurture; after all, someday they would be parents too. **Let other children share in the care of their siblings.**

When my daughter was deciding whether to breast-feed or bottle-feed her baby, I gave her this advice: **"Choose which feeding method is best for you, not which method is more politically correct at the moment."** I wanted her to feel good about whichever method she chose. I had been unable to breast-feed my babies, and initially, the criticism I received from women who didn't understand my circumstances was a source of much frustration and many tears. Unwelcome pressure came from people who were critical of bottle-feeding. I often heard, "Breast-fed babies are more intelligent and healthier," or, "Bottle-fed babies experience less bonding with their mothers." As my babies grew, I realized these hurtful comments were unnecessary and bottle-feeding had been just perfect for me.

A mother of seven says, "I think it's most important to give babies a feeling of warmth and security while they are eating." **Whether you are breast- or bottle-feeding, hold their little bodies close to yours and keep them tightly wrapped.** Most babies love being swaddled while eating.

When breast-feeding, give your baby a bottle once a day to establish flexibility, and try to have someone else give the bottle as often as possible. It is important to introduce your baby to other people and alternative feeding methods. If you're the one who cooks supper at your house, use this time to let Dad or an older sibling feed the baby.

Our baby was premature, weighing less than four pounds. The doctor let us take her home, with explicit instructions: she was to be kept warm and fed warm formula every three hours. He cautioned us to be prepared for a long period of intensive care. We put her at the side of our bed in a basket warmed by a light bulb and warmed her formula as instructed, conscientiously following our doctor's advice. In our zeal to be perfect parents, we never considered changing the regimen as she grew older. Several months later, on an especially hectic day, we gave our precious baby her first cold bottle. Shocked, she took one suck and said, "Warm!" **Trust yourself to put the doctor's advice into perspective as circumstances change.**

I had my doubts about nursing, so it was with much trepidation that I decided to try it. After a month, I realized how much I would be spending if I had to buy formula; I decided to breast-feed for six more months. **Encourage moms, through love and understanding, to breast-feed if they can; they might like it if they try it, or at least discover the significant health and economical advantages it can offer to both mother and baby.**

When I was about to give up on nursing due to cracked nipples, my neighbor suggested I try bag balm, a salve used on dairy cows' udders after milking. It worked wonders and allowed me to continue nursing. Now that I'm a quilter, it also heals my sore fingers overnight! Since 1899, bag balm has been available at craft and quilting stores, drug stores and farm-supply stores. **Use bag balm on dry, cracked or irritated skin.**

*D*oes your baby spit up with feeding? From one mother of a happy spitter to another: **Carry a washcloth that is damp with soda water everywhere.** You'll always be prepared to wipe off anything that is hit, as well as lessen the stench of mother's perfume.

*W*hen my children were about eleven months old and they started knocking the spoon from my hand and throwing food at me, I knew it was time for them to start feeding themselves! I would set the food in front of my child, put a spoon in their hand, and then stand back. **At some point, children must be allowed to practice feeding themselves in order to learn how to do it properly; you might as well start this messy job early.**

Eating is the way to fill up your child's stomach so they will have the energy to do the important work of growing up. **Food should never be used as a punishment or reward.** Giving food as a reward or punishment could lead to eating disorders, obesity, and between-meal snacking that prevents the child from eating regular meals.

My children thought I always served their favorite foods. It was a trick. For example, they said corn was the only vegetable they would eat, so we had green corn (peas), squared corn (cut beans), and big corn (squash). **A little imagination (deception) will overcome many feeding obstacles.**

When I was a young mother in Italy, children were not given solid foods until they started to teethe. At first they were given a piece of home-baked bread to chew or suck on, then they were fed rice cereal and pureed vegetables—and always a teaspoon of olive oil. **Olive oil is practically a cure-all among Italian mothers, but it's especially good for the digestive system and bowels.**

Add a little food coloring to your children's favorite foods—they might get excited about blue pancakes, pink and yellow marbled muffins, or green hard-boiled eggs. **Colors are great attention-getters and make eating more interesting.**

Put a large plastic tablecloth under the high chair. I found it easier to shake off or wipe down a tablecloth than to constantly clean up the floor. It wasn't very attractive; but as with many other inconveniences, I knew this one would only last for a short time.

Present a toddler with a variety of finger foods on his highchair tray. **When the food starts to fly, it usually means the child is full.**

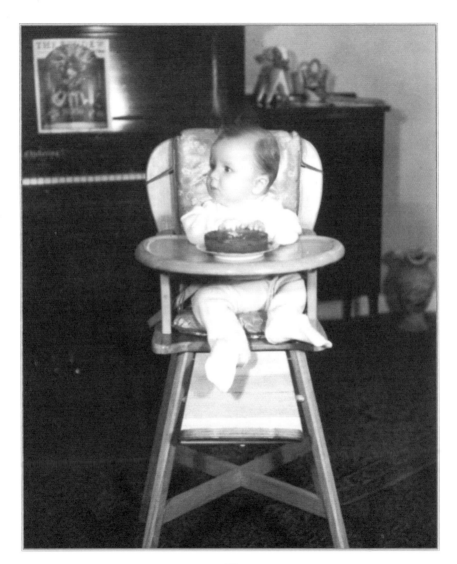

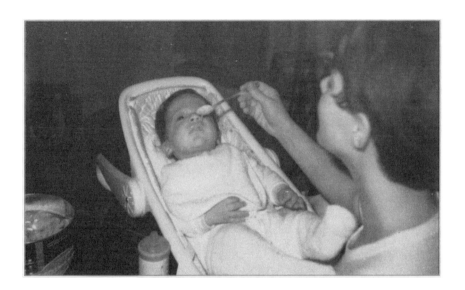

I had a saying posted on my refrigerator for many, many years: **"You have two choices for dinner, take it or leave it."** I did not force my children to eat, but if they chose not to eat when the family was eating, then that was it. There was no short-order grill or bedtime snacks later.

My baby was bottle-fed and loved her milk. When I introduced her to cereal, she spitted, gagged and cried. In desperation, I put a small spoonful of cereal in her mouth, followed immediately by her pacifier. I found out later that this is a tried-and-true trick for introducing thicker, textured foods to a baby's diet. Like most adults, babies have trouble dealing with changes in their routine. **Make changes to your baby's diet slowly, but persistently—even if you have to be tricky.**

Here's my favorite technique for handling children who are too tired, cross, or hungry to be good table companions: invite them to have "supper in the sink." Plop the kids in kitchen sinks filled with warm water and bubbles and serve them their meal there. Frowns turn to laughter as baths and supper are accomplished at the same time. **Bibs are unnecessary and cleanup is easy when kids eat their supper in the sink.** Later, when the children are a bit older and too big for the sink, have special bathtub suppers. Serve the food on a tray and tell stories from your spot on the floor while supervising the eating.

Dr. Rich says:

The two most common questions I get are, "How can I tell if my baby is getting enough milk when I am breast feeding?" and, "Why won't my child eat?" It is good to understand a little physiology to help with the first question. The stomach empties only every three hours or so. If a mother feeds a baby on a one- to two-hour schedule, there is going to be a piling up of milk in the stomach and the baby is going to vomit, and besides that, the mother gets nothing done except feeding the baby. I encourage my mothers to never feed the baby more often than every three hours and to never awaken a baby to feed it. As long as the baby is sleeping, she is not hungry. The average baby will put itself on a very rigid schedule. They will eat when they get hungry. A breast-feeding baby who is getting enough milk will go three to four hours between feedings.

There are two principal reasons for a child to eat poorly. The most common is feeding between meals and the second is drinking too much milk. A mother will come in and say that her two-year old is not eating a thing. I ask her to describe a typical day. I find out that the child skips breakfast; so at ten o'clock, she is hungry and has a cracker or a cookie. By lunchtime, she has already had a cookie, so she is not hungry. At two o'clock, she is hungry again, so she has some chips or candy. Two hours later, dinner is ready and, you guessed it, she is not hungry. Give your child breakfast, lunch, and dinner, and absolutely no between-meal snacks if they are not eating at meal times.

Many mothers ask, "Should I breast- or bottle-feed my baby?" There are two ways of feeding a baby. One is the breast, the other is the bottle. Breast-feeding is not for everyone. Some mothers dislike breast-feeding entirely. The vast majority of babies can do just as well on formulas as they can on breast milk. There are a few advantages to breast-feeding. Breast-fed babies have fewer intestinal track diseases, fewer cases of diarrhea, and some immunity benefits, but not enough to put in your eye. Babies do just about as well on a bottle as on the breast. So, mothers should decide which method works best for her temperament, schedule, and desires.

Basic Formula Recipe

Mix together and warm:

> 18 ounces of water

> 12 ounces evaporated milk

> 1½ tablespoons dark Karo syrup

This formula is especially good for highly allergic babies, but for them, simmer the mixture in a double boiler.

Basic Baby Food Recipe

Vegetables: *Cook up a batch of string beans or peas or squash. Puree them in the blender then freeze in ice-cube trays. When frozen, put cubes in plastic bags. Take out cubes as needed and warm them up.*

Fruits: *Canned or fresh fruit can be used. Puree the fruit in the blender or mash with a fork. Freeze in ice-cube trays and store in plastic bags as with vegetables.*

Solid Food Schedule

This is a sensitive subject because current pediatric guidelines say don't start solid foods until four months. I believe a little cereal augments the baby's contentment and sleeping. But, I also say, if your baby is perfectly satisfied with the breast or the bottle, wait until four months. Cereal first, then two weeks later vegetables, then two weeks later fruits, and then egg yolks, then meats, etc. At six months, the baby has essentially an adult-type digestive system. Most mothers give their babies strained food for the first year. This should be avoided because babies get so hooked on the smooth texture, that, when something lumpy goes down, they vomit. So I tell my mothers when their child reaches six months old, they should open a can of vegetable soup, put some in a bowl, mash it with a fork, and give it to the baby with a spoon. The baby will gag, sputter, and choke, but he won't die. After two to three weeks, the baby will decide he had better like it because that is what he is going to get. By the time the baby is six to seven months of age, he can eat ninety-five percent of what the parents eat.

CHILD CARE HINTS TO REMEMBER

I remember mom saying

_____

_____

My own thoughts

_____

_____

CHAPTER THREE
A Little Something to Suck On

"Most babies give up thumb sucking by the time they get married."
—Homer Rich, M.D.

On our farm was a pigpen with a big sow in it. One day my husband took our toddler out to the pigpen and talked her into throwing her pacifier into the pen so the pig could have something to eat. He was surprised when she actually did it. **The big pig pushed it around and covered it up—no problem with wanting her pacifier after that!**

Because riding in the car provided a pleasant environment for napping, we usually let our toddler have a bottle in his car seat. One day, while riding in the car with the window partially down, he somehow sent his cherished bottle out the window. **Realizing this was an unusual but perfect solution presenting itself, I watched the bottle in the rearview mirror as it bounced down the street.** We waved to the bottle and said, "Bye-bye, bottle, bye-bye."

If all else fails, remember. they will sleep through the night, be potty-trained, get over colic, and quit spitting up before adulthood. **In the meantime, each child is unique and wonderful and deserves our unconditional love, immense patience, and very best efforts.**

*O*ne evening, while putting my daughter to bed, we realized her beloved blankie had been left at my sister's house earlier in the afternoon. Inconsolable, she screamed, "Where is my blankie? I need my blankie!" The entire house was up in alarm, including Grandmamma, who was staying with us. The next day, when my sister returned the blanket, Grandmamma immediately took it and cut it into squares of various sizes, creating enough "blankie cousins" to provide every household in our family with a piece of comfort for my daughter. With a new, reduced-size blanket came words of wisdom from Grandmamma. She told my daughter that since she would be going to school, it was not a good idea to have such a big blankie. However, she would be able to tuck a very small blankie in her school uniform pocket, where only she would know that it was with her. **Often children will accept a grandmother's voice of authority more readily than a parent's.**

I was a thumb-sucker. When I was about five years old, my grandmother said to me, "Quit sucking your thumb or great shovel teeth will grow in your mouth." I didn't really believe that great shovels would grow in my mouth, but my grandmother was a doctor, and I knew that she knew everything, so I stopped immediately. And she was right. My front teeth do protrude.

*O*ur grandma did not believe in thumb-sucking, so she developed a cure. Step one: Using simple food coloring, dip thumb in the dye until colored. Step two: Lightly coat the colored thumb with hot sauce or vinegar. **Once a child tastes something nasty on a food-coloring-coated thumb, only the food coloring is needed the next time to keep the thumb out of the mouth.**

Our first child became very attached to her pacifier. We called it "the shosie," and our family was happy as long as we had shosies in the diaper bag, in her crib, and in every room in the house. All went well until my mother became annoyed that the baby had a pacifier in her mouth most of the time. Mother believed the pacifier would deform her mouth, as well as her teeth. I questioned that logic, and yet I wondered—was I enabling a bad habit? I realized I was not consistent—sometimes I let her have her shosie and sometimes I would refuse to give it to her, which made her very unhappy and confused. After starts and fits and feeling terrible most of the time, my husband said, **"Use your good mothering instincts and decide what you think seems best."** It was a great relief to be reminded that I could deal with this and not ruin my child.

It's the mother's worrying, not the children, that's the biggest problem. Usually a mother's worry about childhood habits is much ado about nothing. Children grow up too soon, and these little annoyances are forgotten.

My mother put a little mustard on my fingers and it stung my tongue. I never sucked my fingers again. **Try a little mustard.**

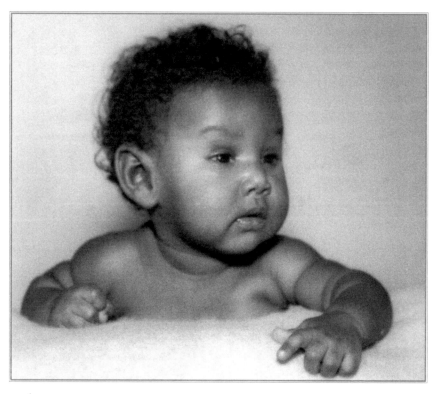

As a thumb-sucker until age eight, I have no solutions. My parents tried Thum liquid, wrapping my thumb with adhesive tape, and other strategies. What finally cured me was a bully. I was contentedly sucking my thumb at school, with my head ducked underneath my desk, when the classroom bully caught sight of me. He was quick to let everyone in the class know that I was a thumb-sucker. **If you can't motivate your child to eliminate bad habits, peer pressure probably will.**

I don't think I was in the room when our dentist explained to our daughter that sucking her thumb was damaging her teeth. But when we got home from that appointment, this serious little child brought her beloved nee-nees, or blankets, to me and told me she couldn't quit sucking her thumb if she had them in her bed. The blankets stayed on the top closet shelf until she was over thumb-sucking. I don't know that I could have taken them away from her, but she reasoned it out and was able to do it by herself. **Try explaining to your child why it's a good idea to stop a bad habit.**

What's wrong with thumb-sucking? I had a friend who made sure all her children sucked their thumbs. She said thumb-suckers are very contented babies, and if they need extra comforting, their thumbs were always close at hand.

Cutting the tips off our granddaughter's pacifiers did not work to wean her from them. We had heard this strategy worked, and maybe it did—for other children. My granddaughter thought it was great fun to stick her fingers in them like they were olives, and she kept right on sucking them, holes and all!

By the time my little girl was two years old, she was sucking her pacifier less and less, so I told her we should throw the pacifier away. **I was surprised at how enthusiastically my daughter threw her pacifier in the trash can when I suggested it.** However, a few minutes later, I saw her go back to the trash can, retrieve the binkie, and suck on it a couple more times. Obviously, my perception of garbage etiquette was not the same as my two-year-old's.

I never took away my children's bottles; instead, I allowed them to give their bottles to Santa's reindeer. We'd package the bottle, address it to the North Pole, take it to the mailbox, and send it away in the slot. Sometimes they would fuss for a night or two and want it back, but I would just say, "Honey, you mailed it to the reindeer to help Santa." It worked seven times for me.

When we lived in Europe, an experienced mother told me that if my baby still had a bottle on his first birthday, I should retire it at the birthday party with great fanfare.

Is there anything more precious than a favorite baby blanket? Maybe not, but clothing? My grandson became attached to a soft, silky robe I wore when he was an infant. He must have bonded with that robe as I rocked him to sleep; he had become used to the feel of this robe and loved it more and more each day. As a toddler, we would often find the robe rolled up beside his pillow. By then, the robe was tattered and his mother wanted to get rid of it; but, fearing that would be too traumatic, we decided to make a small "Hankie" from the fabric before we threw it away. He kept it tucked under his pillow for comfort. Many years later, he took me into his room, reached under his bed, and pulled out a box. Inside was that piece of old robe that had been turned into his Hankie. He said he never wanted to get rid of it because it came from me. **Comfort, security, sentiment—or whatever a blanket is—is priceless.** Why should one ever have to give that up?

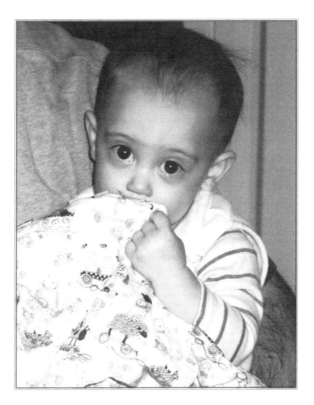

My daughter was two years old and still asking for a bottle at bedtime. When she went with me to visit Grandma, I decided to leave the bottle at home and make a clean break. **When bedtime came, she asked for her bottle; I told her I didn't have one and neither did Grandma—we even checked Grandma's cupboards.** I was worried she would be upset, but she accepted the situation; and, when we returned home, the bottles were gone there too.

Dr. Rich says:

The Pacifier is a very good thing for the first three or four months. *It develops the muscles in the jaw. I recommend that mothers take the pacifier away by six months before children get hooked on it, and take them off the bottle by a year. I hate to see a child walking around the house at age two with a bottle in his hand. Start the baby on a cup at nine months. By the time they are a year old, they can drink just fine out of a cup. If the child is hooked on the bottle or pacifier, I tell the mother to take a pair of scissors and cut off the top of the pacifier and the nipples on the bottles and then plan on having about three very difficult days and nights. But then it is done.*

Thumb-sucking is a different matter, and a pacifier will not prevent thumb-sucking. Babies get some sort of subconscious satisfaction from thumb-sucking. It doesn't hurt them, and trying to make them stop only frustrates them. If it nauseates you, then turn your head.

One of the most disastrous things a mother can do is let her baby go to sleep with the bottle. Having a bottle in the mouth all night promotes poor dental hygiene and tooth decay. I tell mothers not to prop up the bottle for the baby or let the baby go to sleep with the bottle. Feed the baby, then put the baby down.

CHILD CARE HINTS TO REMEMBER

I remember mom saying

_____

_____

My own thoughts

_____

_____

CHAPTER FOUR

Rubber Duckies, Bubbles & Other Magic Tricks

"We all bathe too often."
—Homer Rich, M.D.

With the birth of our tiny premature twin girls, my husband and I found ourselves the parents of four children under the age of four. We were thrilled and overwhelmed. My type-A personality kicked in and I began to set things straight. My fetish for cleanliness and organization would save the day. With so many young children, we made many visits to our friendly, concerned pediatrician. He was a low-key, cowboy kind of guy with boots and all. On one visit, he took a look at us and said that mom looked worse than the sick kids. He pointed to the children's binkies and bottles and said, "My word! Are those bottles and pacifiers color-coded?" I guess I did look frazzled, but I had to keep these kids healthy and germ free! In defense I began to babble about how happy I was to have found a great tape that came in four colors. The four-year-old's things were labeled blue, the seventeen-month-old's red, and the twin girls' were green and yellow. "Let me guess," he said, "You probably wash all their diapers separately too—am I right?" He explained that I was going to keel over from exhaustion if I kept it up—he had seen how germs travel through the ventilation systems of hospitals at lightening speed, and I didn't stand much chance against the war I was fighting in a regular home environment. After some soul searching, I decided that my time would be better spent hugging each child more and using my cleaning and labeling energy elsewhere. **Although cleanliness is important, it is not more important than spending quality time with your children.**

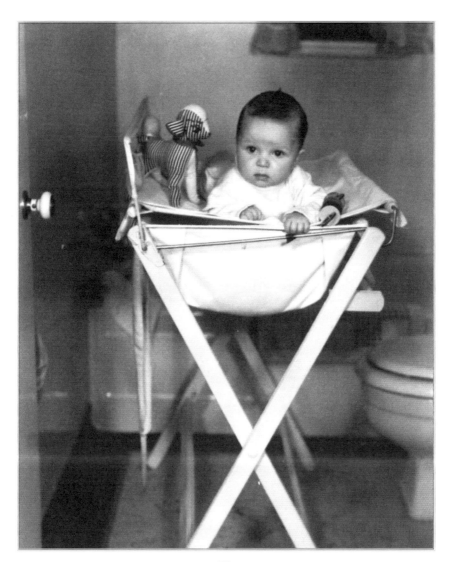

When I took my children out of the tub, I would pretend they were babies again and wrap them up in towels, bouncing them and sing "Rock-a-Bye Baby" and a Swiss-German song about drizzling rain called, "Rita, Rita, Restle." **Bath time is one of the most nurturing, uncomplicated, happy times we spend with our children.**

In the hot, dry climate of the reservation, my Native American grandmother bathed her babies in a tin baking dish. And since the water had to be hauled by hand, she only did it every other day or so. **There is no right or wrong way to bathe a baby; after all, bathing traditions differ from culture to culture.**

Three of my sons had tubes in their ears because of numerous ear infections. I found putting Silly Putty in their ears kept the water out during bath time. The only kind I could find was the glow-in-the-dark variety. We used to turn out the lights and watch their ears glow. **Silly Putty can help children who are prone to ear infections or swimmer's ear by keeping water out of their ears.**

Children's tastes differ as much as adults'. Some like quick baths, some like to soak, some like showers, but most do not. In any case, bath time is a good time for unhindered communication with your child. **Talk to your children about water and how water helps us feel calm and relaxed.** They will learn to enjoy bathing and to feel comfortable and safe in the water.

A rubber duckie, bubbles, motorboat and a song, Three Men in a Tub—these toys made bath time a time for fun, smiles and laughter. Taking my baby out of the tub and wrapping him up in a warm towel, rubbing him down with lotion and having that precious bundle smiling up at me was one of my greatest joys. **Enjoy the heart-warming experience of bathing your baby while you can.**

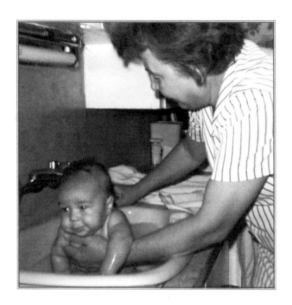

When my children didn't want to get washed, I would say, "Let's make a soapy man!" **I would lather their little bodies with bubbles and then let them dunk under the water to rinse.** They loved it.

Most children love to bathe in the kitchen sink. I don't know whether it's because they're perched up high and can survey the world around them or because the tight space is comforting. I watched my grandmother, dressed in a work apron, bathe her grandchildren in the sink, and now I bathe my grandchildren the same way. A visit to grandma's house is just not the same without a bath in the sink.

Bathe the baby surrounded by siblings. It gives the baby a chance to feel part of the group and older children to be part of the baby's life.

I knew a woman who bathed her children every night, but very seldom washed their bedding. **What good does it do to take a bath every night and not have clean sheets to lie on?**

Establish a toothbrushing routine—allow the children to brush first, then follow up with a brushing to make sure they haven't missed anything. **The secret to healthy teeth is consistency.**

A good way to introduce toothbrushing is to give a small toothbrush to the baby to play with in the tub. Under your supervision, let a trickle of water run; they can learn to brush and spit to their heart's content without making a mess.

Our daughters liked to play beauty shop in the bathtub. They washed each other's hair, fashioning the soapy hair into wildly contorted styles, then rinsing under the faucet. Afterward, I helped them blow-dry and brush their hair while they admired themselves in the bathroom mirror. They never seemed to get tired of this routine. **Instill a sense of comfort and fun during bath time, and children will follow your example.**

Mothers in Vietnam, like mothers everywhere, often use special treatments and techniques that are unique to their culture. I have many memories of my mother taking care of me and my siblings, but one of the fondest is the tropical smell of coconut. My mother added coconut milk to our bath water to make the water soft and sweet smelling; the scent remains with me to this day.

You don't have to bathe your children in the tub; they might feel safer in small quarters. **In my day, we bathed every Saturday night in a #3 galvanized tub—girls first!**

Bath-bottle-bed is an ideal nighttime routine for young children. My mother and father always shared parenting responsibilities; their bath-bottle-bed routine has become a tradition in our family. Whether we do the whole schedule together or split the duties, having a united front turns one of the most stressful times of a busy day into one of the most enjoyable and rewarding. As the children get older, they learn not to whine or moan when Mom or Dad says it's time for bath bottle-bed.

Gentle baby soap and shampoo turn little ones into sweet-smelling, snuggly creatures, which encourage lots of hugs and kisses; and we all need plenty of that! **Until babies are out of diapers, daily baths are necessary.**

A pediatric nurse told me that swabbing alcohol on a newborn's umbilical cord doesn't hurt them—they just flinch because it feels cold. The same nurse also said that the very safest way to trim a tiny baby's nails is to bite them off. I tried it and it really works! **Practical little hints from professional caregivers can relieve the apprehension many new mothers feel with their first baby.**

Dr. Rich says:

Mothers tend be overly conscientious—they keep the room temperature too high, cover the baby with too many blankets, and then wonder why their baby is screaming and has a rash. **Babies have the same temperature regulators as we do. If the room is too warm for you, the baby is probably uncomfortable; if you feel chilly, the baby probably needs another blanket.**

A baby's skin gets dried out from too much soap and bathing. *A daily clear water bath is usually sufficient; only use soap once or twice a week. Baby oils and lotion tend to shut down the baby's natural oils, which can also lead to dry skin, so they should be used sparingly, if at all.*

When baby teeth first appear, put a wet washcloth on your finger and clean them. **When the baby is about eighteen months old, you can introduce them to the harsher toothbrush.**

Mothers should not be afraid to submerge their babies in the water. *With their gentle encouragement, babies learn to hold their breath and not be frightened of the water.*

Don't worry, nature takes care of the umbilical cord. *It is almost impossible to keep it dry because of the diaper, but dabbing with alcohol keeps the mother busy.*

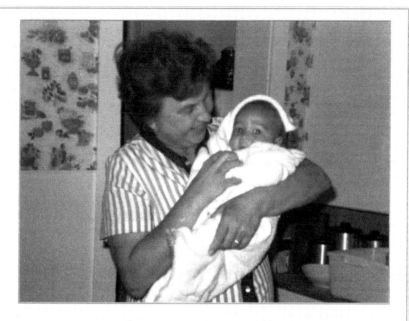

CHILD CARE HINTS TO REMEMBER

I remember mom saying

_____

_____

My own thoughts

_____

_____

CHAPTER FIVE
Getting Some Shut-eye

"I tell the mother to turn her antenna one-quarter turn
so that she doesn't hear the baby hollering."
—Homer Rich, M.D.

I became so distressed listening to my first baby cry that I began rocking him until he fell asleep before laying him down in his crib. I loved doing that, but soon realized I was spending a good portion of my day in the rocking chair. I wanted him to be able to get himself to sleep; but in the back of my mind I thought that, if I left him alone to cry, he would think I no longer loved him and would be emotionally damaged. One morning, as I was rocking him to sleep, the phone rang. I put him in his crib to answer the phone. It was a friend who would not let me hang up. As I finally said good-bye, I realized my baby had quit crying. I hovered over the crib, afraid he had experienced trauma from crying so long; but when he awoke, he was happy and glad to see me. I had discovered that my baby could fall to sleep on his own. It wasn't this easy every day—some days were definitely harder than others. But my advice is to let your child cry for about five minutes, then peek in to assure yourself he's not hurt or injured. If all is well, let him cry five more minutes. If he is still crying hard, go in and hold him to calm him down and then try again. **With a little perseverance, babies can learn to fall asleep alone.**

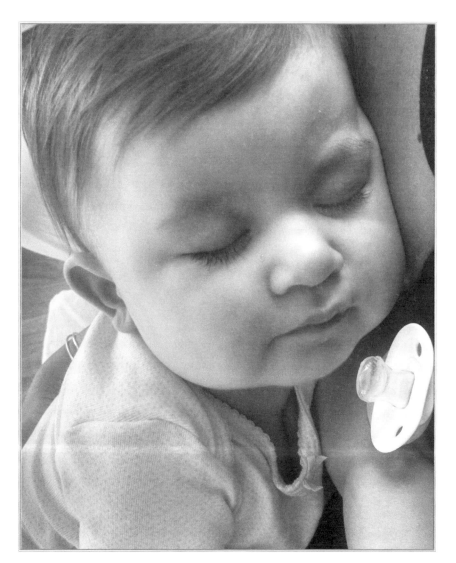

Most children reach a point when they want to have more control over how, when, and where they will sleep. To get past this stubbornness, my grandmother played a game with me and my brother—we were to see who could keep their eyes closed the longest. We fell asleep every time. **Grandmothers are very tricky when it comes to getting children to do what they want them to.**

I found that being regular and putting children to bed at the same time, in the same place—with love, happiness and care for their well-being—was the most important part of getting them to sleep. The first night I put our firstborn on a schedule my husband complained, "I can't stand to hear her cry." I responded, "Then you go take a walk while she goes to sleep." The second night she cried for about forty minutes. The third night she cried just fifteen minutes. From then on, when we put her in her crib, she was happy and went to sleep without any crying. She had a good night's rest and so did we. Babies do not know what is expected of them unless we teach them. **Developing sleeping habits will not only make the baby more healthy and well-balanced, but the parents as well.**

One of the best reasons to breast-feed is that it presents a legitimate reason to lay down together for a nap. My children and I would all lie down together—one at the breast, one with a book, and one with a treasure to hold. We all fell asleep in a loving jumble. I learned the treasure trick from my mother. In a nearby drawer, assemble a collection of interesting items for the children to inspect and hold during naptime only. Try small mirrors, compacts, fingernail kits, or large costume jewelry. Children are distracted by this quiet activity and are soon relaxed and ready to sleep. **Creative control techniques help establish mommy-friendly naptime schedules.**

I don't remember fighting with my children about naptime because we had a fairly strict sleeping schedule. They always liked their beds and were only in them when they were tired. **If you want your child to enjoy bedtime, never use the bed as a punishment or a containment area.**

Each one of my children had unique sleep needs. Some were good sleepers and had no trouble falling and staying asleep. Others needed to cuddle up against my body all night long. I let my babies dictate what their comfort zone was and never imposed my will on them. **I believe that contented, relaxed babies make better sleepers right from the start.**

When nothing else seemed to put my baby to sleep, my husband and I would take our baby in the car and go for a short ride. **The sound and vibration of the car's engine never failed to put our little one to sleep.**

Babies don't need lots of blankets and layers of clothes. These create uncomfortable bulkiness and an uneven temperature—the baby's body can get miserably overheated while the head is still cool. **When your baby is cranky at night, make the room a little warmer so you can dress her a little lighter.**

Having my baby sleep through the night for the first time was almost scary. The first time it happened, I woke up, looked at the clock, and realized in a panic the baby had not cried. I hurried frantically to the crib, knowing something must be wrong; but as I looked into the crib, I found my son sleeping peacefully. With relief, I tiptoed back to bed, hoping not to wake him so that I could sleep even longer. Other times, I'd toss and turn in bed, sure he would wake up any minute. Finally I decided to just stay up and try to accomplish a few more things, disregarding my mother's advice: "Just go to bed when your baby goes down." **I should have listened to my mother and left the chores for another day and gone to bed with my child.**

Vietnamese mothers swing their babies in hammocks to calm them. **If you don't have a hammock, soothe a baby with the repetitive, gentle motion of a baby swing.**

I had no children of my own, but I inherited step-children who, in later years, blessed me with four wonderful grandchildren. The first started to stay with us when she was less than two months old. What a joy to wake up with this tiny baby swaddled up in our bed! Yes, she slept with us—and continued to do so until she was three years old or more. The first few times she slept over, I didn't sleep much; between feeding, changing, and worrying, I didn't have time. But grandpa, having already raised three children, wanted her close to us and I have priceless memories of those times. **It was lovely to experience, even secondhand, the incredibly powerful feelings a baby brings into your life.** Of course, I always knew the baby would soon return to her mother and I would have a good night's sleep again.

Learning to sleep through the night is a gradual process. Don't try to get your newborn to sleep from 7 P.M. till morning. Instead, give him a bath at 10:30 P.M., have some one-on-one time together, and then fill his tummy up. After he's been stimulated and fed, put him down for the night. It works best to train the baby to sleep the midnight-to-morning shift first.

My Jewish grandmother quipped, "Play, bathe—do anything to keep the child awake for two hours before bedtime." A baby who naps in the evening is less likely to sleep through the night than an exhausted baby.

"Sole, Sole" (pronounced soul-lee), a lullaby brought from Switzerland by my grandmother, has been a very special part of raising children in my family. The two-word lullaby can be sung to the tune of any child's song. The soft sound of "Sole, Sole" seems to calm, soothe, and relax babies. Some of my fondest memories were created as I rocked my children and grandchildren to sleep, singing this lullaby. Grandmothers everywhere seem to celebrate this tradition of singing and rocking.

I questioned my doctor about the pros and cons of having our infant sleep in our bed. He said that about half of all newborns sleep with their parents. But he cautioned that if a baby is in an adult bed, that bed should not have a pillow-top mattress and all pillows and fluffy coverings should be removed. He also mentioned that a good night's sleep would be rare for the couple that chooses this arrangement. Carefully consider whether or not to let your baby sleep in bed with you.

Cradleboards have many advantages for Native American mothers and their babies. They are portable and a great convenience for mothers who must keep on the go. **Native American babies become so used to sleeping tightly wrapped on a cradleboard that it is hard for them to sleep any other way.**

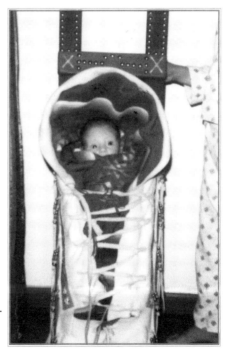

In Hawaii, mothers feed their babies a little Poi after their last feeding in the evening. Like cereal, poi helps keep babies' tummies full during the night so they sleep better. While some adults don't like the taste of poi, many Hawaiians, who are introduced to the taste as infants, grow up loving it.

If you want your baby to sleep through the night, offer them a bottle of very thin rice cereal at about nine o'clock in the evening. They won't wake up hungry in the middle of the night.

My mother had a marvelous way of keeping newborns cozy. She swaddled the baby in a light blanket, feet and arms tucked in tightly, and topped its head with a tiny stocking cap to keep the heat in. Then she laid the baby on its side, its back propped up by a small towel rolled up like a hotdog. Mother called the towel a cousin—the cousin would keep the baby company as he or she slept. **Babies feel more secure when they're warm and snug.**

Once I prepared for a party at my home, I discovered that my baby was soothed by the sound of the vacuum. I had avoided vacuuming for fear it would scare my infant; but, to my surprise, the very sound I had avoided lulled him to sleep. **Don't be afraid to experiment.**

Nothing induces sleep better than a small pillow or stuffed animal placed lightly over a toddler's eyes combined with a lulling voice. I found that a child who listens in the darkness to a very long prayer or story will quickly fall asleep.

Dr. Rich says:

Most babies come home from the hospital with their days and nights mixed up. Try to keep them awake during the day as much as you can. They will be so tired that, by nine o'clock in the evening, they will be ready to sleep at night. About two days like that and the baby is turned around. I have never read that in a book—I just learned it from experience.

I have always recommended that babies can stay in a bassinet until about three months—or until they kick out the end of it.

Babies will start sleeping through the night when they are ready. It is entirely up to them. The average baby starts sleeping through the night at six to eight months of age. At eight months, the mother should be able to feed the baby, put her in the crib, and say goodnight. If the baby wakes up in the night to eat and is well and of normal size, I tell the mother to turn her antenna one-quarter turn so that she doesn't hear the baby. She may cry up to an hour. After two nights, maybe three, the baby will realize that she is not going to be fed and will start sleeping through the night. There is no reason for a normal, healthy baby to be waking up two, three, four times a night. After trying this method, most mothers come back to me and thank me for teaching them how to get their babies to sleep through the night and for making their homes happy again.

There is a trend nowadays for the kids to sleep with their parents in one great big bed. For their safety, and for normal emotional and sexual development, children should sleep in their own beds. Everyone sleeps better in their own bed.

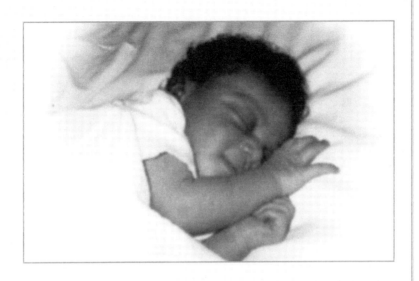

CHILD CARE HINTS TO REMEMBER

I remember mom saying

_____

_____

My own thoughts

_____

_____

CHAPTER SIX
Cry, Baby, Cry

"The average baby needs to cry about one and one-half
hours every day for exercise."
—Homer Rich, M.D.

As a first-time mom, I took crying very seriously. Every time my first child cried I immediately responded with hugs, kisses and sympathy. Once I had two or three kids, however, I didn't have time to run every time one of them cried. So I learned to recognize the different kinds of cries: the sob that meant their feelings were hurt, the wail that said "I'm angry," or the urgent scream that meant they were physically hurt. But the cry I really learned to watch out for was the one that children used to get attention. My mother-in-law taught me a great technique that turned attention-getting crying into laughter every time. Say to the crying child, "Come over here and I will pick you up." If they can walk, they're not hurt very badly and they will soon realize that the joke is on them. **Humor—yours and your child's—can get families past many rough spots, especially episodes of unnecessary crying!**

All babies are good; some just cry more than others. **"Crying is nature's way of letting babies get out bad or sad thoughts so they can sleep better," says Grandma.** Of course, ignoring the crying is the adult's responsibility—keep yourself busy by vacuuming or cleaning the shower.

We once had a mother and her little boy living with us. The boy woke up every morning crying. I began to listen for his stirrings and rush into his room before he could start crying and get him right up. I'd give him a love and the attention he needed to begin his day. Soon he no longer woke up crying. I believe the boy's mother had unknowingly conditioned her baby to cry whenever he wanted her because she never paid any attention to him until he cried. **Wouldn't it be better if all babies received the emotional warmth and trust they need without demanding it?**

It is a myth that a good mother always knows why her baby is crying—don't let this myth bother you. Some mothers even torture themselves with the fallacy that chronic crying is a result of poor bonding. This is absolutely not true! Most babies go through difficult periods of crying. If you're baby's crying is driving you crazy, put the baby in a safe place and leave the room or pass him to someone else. **Crying never hurt a baby, but frustrated adults have.**

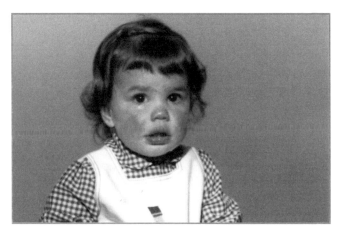

As a grandmother, my years of experience have taught me to repeat this truth in times of stress, "This too shall pass." Sometimes it is difficult for parents to take the long view when they're in the middle of what seems like a crisis. The dramas of small children can bring parents to laughter or tears on a daily basis. I urge them to lean toward laughter, because most of the little upsets will turn out to be much ado about nothing in the grand scheme of things.

I came from a very disciplined military family. This environment taught my mother to use defensive strategies to distract her children before they started to cry. **My mother said it was better to avoid the crying than to reward it with attention.**

I was always experimenting with ways to calm my first child when he cried. I found out, quite by accident, that he calmed down to the sound of running water. So, when he was upset, we'd go into the bathroom and turn on a faucet. I wished I could put a comfortable chair in the bathroom so we could be relaxed together! **Think about using soothing sounds such as running water, a whirling fan, or heartbeat music to promote a calming environment for your baby.**

Hold newborns tightly to your chest so they can hear your heartbeat, and whisper sweet nothings to distract them from crying.

*Y*ou will know how old I am when I tell you about my experience with calming down a crying baby. I was already the mother of three children when our last son was born, and I believed I had the crying thing down pat. I was past having guilt pangs when my children cried and thought they had all adapted very well to the schedule and discipline I had established. Then our fourth baby was born; right from the start, he was a superior crier. He required much more holding and rocking than the others. I became anxious about spending so much time with just one of my children and tired from trying to give the other children what they needed. My husband was as helpful as he could be and encouraged me to give my time and attention to this baby who needed me so much. One day he surprised me with the latest and greatest invention—a small black-and-white television set and a genuine La-Z-Boy rocker. He hoped this would help me relax while taking care of my fussy baby. He was right. Not only did the rocking make the baby content, but my anxiety melted away with the sounds from that amazing new invention. **Learn to gratefully accept help from others; there are no prizes for the mother who does it all.**

Sometimes crying is the result of a serious injury; more often than not, however, the injuries are minor or even imaginary. When I suspected the crying was probably for effect, I gave the little patient three choices: we could go to the doctor, cut off the sore part, or kiss it better and put a bandage on it. Most often, they chose the latter option. Another good trick is to draw their attention to the thing that hurt them; for instance, inspect the wall they ran into or the toy they tripped over. Make sure the wall is not dented or bruised or the toy damaged. Children will quickly forget what they were crying about if they are distracted in this way.

Because I never had children of my own, I probably looked at crying differently than most grandmas. **To me, crying was an excuse to hold, cuddle and experience the joy I had missed.**

A high-strung daughter with her first baby reminded us quickly of what it means to be a new mother. Our new addition was extremely fussy, crying much of the time. We tried everything, but nothing seemed to soothe him. After many sleepless nights, the doctors discovered he had several problems that would require medication, special formula, devoted care, and most of all, patience. One evening, after a particularly stressful day, my daughter appeared at my door, holding a squirming bundle out to me, and said, "Here, I don't want to be a mother anymore!" As luck would have it, six of my closest friends were at my home that evening and they heard my daughter's frustrated outburst. Well, nothing gets a grandmother going like a plea for help with a baby. Seven grandmothers leaped into action to take charge of the baby and buoy up my exhausted daughter. With a little help and encouragement, my grandson grew out of his problems to become a very delightful little boy. **Loving, supportive grandmothers and other mothers can provide invaluable help to new mothers during tough times—just ask them.**

When our children had trouble settling down, we took them strolling through the neighborhood. They seemed to love the rhythm of walking and the cool night air. Or we would sit outside on the porch steps and sing softly in the night air. "Little Bobby Shaftoe" was one song I remember my own mother singing to me. **Walking or singing rhythmic songs has a calming effect, especially if you can do it out in the fresh air—babies love to be outside.**

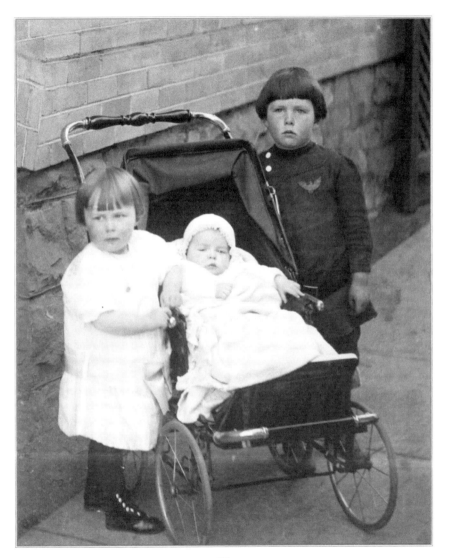

*O*ur granddaughter was born six weeks early with respiratory complications and other health issues. She was very small, about the size of a Sunday roast, her grandmother said. In the following months, she endured several serious episodes that kept her mother and us in a constant state of apprehension. When the baby was seven months old, I went to stay with her and my daughter in their tiny apartment. I slept in my daughter's room with her, and the baby slept in the next room, in her crib. All through the night, I lay awake, listening to horrible choking sounds coming from my precious granddaughter. I was positive she would not make it through the night. I whispered to my sleepy daughter, "How can you listen to your darling daughter die and not try to do anything to help her?" Although it was a heartless comment to make to a young mom, she gently explained that over the course of the last few months, she had come to know her daughter's sounds very well. She could easily identify the sounds that were relatively normal, given the baby's respiratory condition, and also the sounds that signaled trouble. She assured me that although it sounded bad, my granddaughter was actually doing pretty well at the moment. Parenting is often fun and wonderful, but it can also be hard and scary. **Miraculously, mothers come to know their children in ways that are hard for others to understand.** It is a special bond that allows them to communicate at the most basic levels.

I could tell if the crying were sincere by whether or not tears were present. I would find out what the problem was if tears were being shed. If there were no tears, I would let them cry until they got tired and stopped.

Dr. Rich says:

*Why do babies cry? To determine why your baby is crying, follow these steps. First, assess the situation. Is your baby sick? Is your baby hungry or have an upset tummy? Is your baby wet? Is your baby tired? Does your baby need more attention? Second, try your best to solve these problems. Third, realize that babies are very good at manipulating their parents. So, listen to your instincts, be calm, and don't panic. Crying is what babies do best. **Remember, even the most patient and calm parents feel upset when their child won't stop crying.***

CHILD CARE HINTS TO REMEMBER

I remember mom saying

_____

_____

My own thoughts

_____

_____

CHAPTER SEVEN
Naughty or Nice?

"Every baby is a law unto itself."
—Homer Rich, M.D.

My brothers and I came rather late into our parents' lives and we were absolutely adored. We were not, however, spoiled. One day when I was having a little trouble with my own young son, my father offered these prophetic words of advice: "He can pay now, or you can pay later." That truism has been proven over and again to me as I watched my children, and now my grandchildren, struggle for independence. Discipline is sometimes painful, but it is necessary. **Rules that are established and enforced while children are young will often prevent much greater heartache later.**

We had one daughter who's personality seemed to require temper tantrums, so we just let her have them. We only had one condition—she had to lie down on the floor in front of the refrigerator. Before long, I began to notice a correlation between tantrums and being tired or hungry. If I fed her and made sure she was rested, the tantrums would disappear. It was not just bad temper with her; her behavior had definite physical causes, as I suspect may be the case with many children. **So often we blame our children's behavior on their naughty natures or stubbornness when, in fact, there may be causes that the child does not have much control over.** With a little insight, we can help them change their behavior for the better.

Is there a situation more frightening to parents than a child who holds his breath during temper tantrums? If your child does this, try this trick. **Blow into the toddler's mouth, as if you were doing CPR, until he starts breathing.** I don't know if it's the shock or the air, but it works great!

You can take it from a grandmother and teacher with over twenty years of experience—children who have been raised in a home where there is structure, where family rules are respected by all, and where each family member is given responsibilities will do better in school and in life. **Consistency in responsibility, as well as discipline, is the key.**

In rural, southern Italy over a half century ago, people did not have the child-rearing information or skills of today. We were poor, most of us illiterate, and we just did as our parents and grandparents did before us. A "time-out" was unknown as a form of discipline; we only knew spanking. So that's what I did when I thought my children were really out of control. **How lucky today's moms are to have modern research so readily available in books, magazines and on the internet to help them make informed decisions about their child's care.**

In my day, when Mom laid down the law, it was either, "Go to your room until I tell you to come out," or, "Sit on that chair until I tell you to get down." **You don't need to use trendy or complicated schemes for discipline to be effective.**

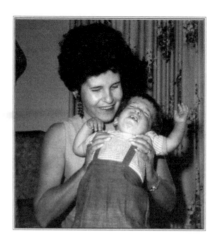

*D*ealing with a temper tantrum in public is inconvenient at best; but no matter how annoying they are, temper tantrums must be dealt with immediately to change the unacceptable behavior. Swiftly and firmly remove the child to a place where you can talk about what they want, why it is important, and what to do about getting it or not getting it. **Do not give in to an act of defiance, or you will find yourself with a major problem when it is least convenient.**

*W*ith a houseful of boys, I could always count on a couple of them to be squabbling. **A quick and effective cooling-off period can be achieved by sitting the culprits back-to-back on stools, where they can be easily supervised.** Usually it won't take long for them to be laughing and cooperative again.

My grandfather believed a spoonful of discipline goes a long way. He would fill a teaspoon with water and, flipping the handle, send the contents of the spoon across the room into the face of the surprised offender. I always wondered how long he had to practice to aim with such amazing accuracy. If we lingered too long after a reminder for bedtime, a well-placed splatter sent us scattering to our rooms. We knew it was half in fun, but we also knew he meant it. The trick was especially handy for cooling off an argument that was getting a bit too heated. Grandfather was usually so sly that we rarely saw him dip his spoon into a glass and poise it for action. **The effectiveness of the formidable spoon discipline was the element of surprise.** Combined with the look on Grandfather's face, the technique was enough to immediately change behavior.

As a mother and as a teacher, I believe children should learn something from the discipline they get—something that enforces the values they will take with them into adulthood. **If the discipline enhances or encourages poor behaviors instead of reinforcing good ones, try other forms of discipline until you find one that's not counterproductive.**

My grandmother always told me to choose my battles wisely and sparingly. You can't discipline a child for every little thing or the discipline will lose its effectiveness. Constant discipline will only cause hard feelings and can result in aggressive behavior.

Completely ignore the first temper tantrum and you will save yourself a lot of time and trouble.

The thing I notice about the mothers I admire is that they are kind, but firm. A consistently firm attitude will foster a sense of right and wrong in the child that will allow them to monitor and control their own behavior. **Teaching children to control themselves empowers them and prevents excessive conflict between parent and child.**

Often parents give children the opportunity to make decisions before they are ready or capable of making those judgments. For example, a mother might ask her young daughter to decide, out of all her clothes, what to wear. The daughter is probably too young to understand how to choose tasteful, sensible outfits. Instead, she would let her choose between two things, asking, "Do you want to wear this dress or that one?" **Let your child choose between two right options as you start to teach them the concept of making correct choices.**

Listen to children. Be respectful of their thoughts and allow them to make as many decisions as possible on their own so they learn to reason things through. **Children can learn from small consequences before they are old enough to face huge consequences.** Common sense goes a long way.

Talk, talk, talk, and explain, explain, explain to your children. If you

speak to children in a clear, sensible way, they will know what is expected of them, and, more importantly, why. **Always tell the truth and never threaten a consequence you are not prepared to follow through with.** In this way, they will learn to trust you and your judgment.

Children must learn self-discipline; what better place to start learning than at home. During the first few months, you must babyproof your home by eliminating potentially dangerous situations and putting fragile or harmful objects out of reach. As the baby becomes a toddler, start teaching the concept of self-discipline by introducing no and off-limits; however, make sure you present an acceptable alternative, such as an interesting object that can be called a yes object, which can be touched and handled.

My girls tell me that I was the meanest mother, but they sure are glad now

that I was. They say they still remember the look that meant they had better stop whatever they were doing and that when I snapped my fingers, they knew they had received their very last warning. **My philosophy was, I am the boss.**

It seems harsh now, but I put my children in their rooms and let 'em cry! In their anger, they sometimes emptied every drawer and overturned the furniture in their rooms. I didn't let this pull me off course because I knew it just meant they would also have a mess to clean up before they could come out.

When a grandchild misbehaves in my home, I simply say, "We don't do that at grandma's house." Of course, there is also a lot of give and take at Grandma's house; sometimes they can break one of their parents' rules, such as staying up late or eating in bed, when they are with Grandma. **Usually, a little well-placed leniency encourages them to go along with the rest of Grandma's rules.**

Some children are more afraid of one parent than the other. Our children were a little more scared of their dad than me. I didn't always like it, but occasionally it really helped to have effective backup support, especially when the kids were teenagers, since teenagers will push the limits. **A little fear never hurt anyone.**

Dr. Rich says:

Temper tantrums are a means for babies and children to let off steam and try to get what they want. When the child is about eighteen months old, there are several methods of managing temper tantrums. One is the "time-out" method. Bodily pick up the child and put them in a bedroom or in a corner and say, "When you simmer down, you can come out." Another way is to completely ignore the tantrum. If the screaming doesn't stop, close the door and let them scream. He will simmer down after a while and everything will be fine. Many books and articles are didactic and theoretical but not proven clinically, as far as I am concerned. It is easy for a new mother to become confused and not know what to do. She has to learn by experience and consistency is the key.

CHILD CARE HINTS TO REMEMBER

I remember mom saying

_____

_____

My own thoughts

_____

_____

CHAPTER EIGHT
Get Ready, Get Set, Go!

"Mothers know best."
—Homer Rich, M.D.

As a baby becomes a toddler and a toddler becomes a child, new parents become aware of a whole new set of challenges. **This chapter deals with the three growing-up issues we hear mothers worry about the most**—potty-training, anatomy training, and traveling.

As adults, we sometimes assume children have a greater understanding of vocabulary and situations than they do. We have two granddaughters who are quite close in age. While the older one was potty-trained, she still wore a diaper to bed. When the little sister was potty-training, she just stopped wearing diapers cold turkey—day and night. One night when they were getting ready for bed, the older one commented that the younger one was wearing her unders to bed instead of a diaper. Her mom reminded her that she wore a diaper to bed because she was still waking up wet, while her younger sister was not. After the discussion, her mother asked her, "Do you think you could start waking up dry?" She answered, "Sure," and that was it. Our granddaughter hadn't understood why she was wearing a diaper to bed and no one had thought to explain it to her.

It is hard to tell how to be successful at potty-training because each child is so different. After seven children, I can tell you that with each one, potty training was an adventure! As my children approached the age of two, I started planning for potty-training—that was just the age that it was done in those days. When my seventh child approached the magic age, I tried a book someone had recommended to me that had instructions on how to potty-train in one day. I struggled to find a place for my six other children to spend the day because the book said that you had to be alone with the child you were potty-training. I found myself alone with my youngest in the bathroom, armed with a dolly that wet and a plethora of tasty snacks, soda pop, juice, and water. We fed the dolly water and had her go in the potty to show my little girl how it was done. I also fed my child crackers, cookies and plenty of juice, water and soda which was supposed to help her go to the potty just like the dolly did. After spending a couple of hours doing this with no success, my little girl looked up at me and said, "Mommy, my throat feels funny," and then she threw up all the snacks and drinks. Needless to say, that was the end of that. I don't think there is a short cut to potty-training.

If a toddler still has a bottle before bed, they are probably not going to wake up dry. **Taking away the bottle before attempting to potty-train makes sense.**

My husband said, "If they're still in diapers when they start school, you can teach them to change their own!"

This is an unusual potty training method, if you don't mind a soggy vacation. When we were ready to introduce the potty, we took our children on a trip and told them that since we were away from home, the "diaper man" would not be able to find us. The children asked, "How do we get some more diapers?" We replied, "We can't—you'll just have to use the potty." **Children will adapt to new situations when given a line of reasoning.**

Little boy's mechanics don't seem to mature as early as little girl's. I know this sounds silly, but to help them practice control, I'd allow them to go outside and see how far they could squirt. With five boys, I tried to make everything a contest.

I simply called urinating "going to the bathroom." I fully realize that people go into the bathroom to do many other things besides urinating, but I still don't think it's necessary to be so descriptive. **"Going to the bathroom" seems to be a more polite way of explaining yourself to others.**

I must confess I was more of the old school. **We used general terms for body parts—your "bottom" covered a fairly wide range of body parts in the nether region.** My adult children are much more descriptive when talking to the grandchildren.

Proper anatomical names, used in wholesome context, were the standard in our family, but travel—exposure to the outside world—can cast a comic light on a family's standards. When we were stationed in Oslo, Norway, our six- and eight-year-old boys were enrolled in a small private school for embassy children, where six languages were spoken by the children. Our boys collected an extensive vocabulary of anatomy that sent them into giggles, and a few choice examples remain with our family to this day. I am certain they were not anatomical correct terms in any language, but I don't believe their use had any negative effect on IQ, educational achievement, or moral character.

<hr/>

Six of our sons were born in less than eight years, and we did a lot of traveling nationally and internationally. When they were young, I dressed all the boys in the same brightly colored shirts because it enabled me to count them quickly in busy airports. We also had a buddy system. Each older boy was responsible for a younger brother. **Easily identifiable clothing and the buddy system kept my family safe and organized.**

<hr/>

When traveling in the car, play recognition games. One game is to watch signs for alphabet letters; start with A until someone finds the letter A on a sign, then move to B and so forth. Another is "I spy the colors"—one child spies something red and others guess what it is. The winner then spies another colorful object. Older children can also recognize license plates and see how many states they can find. Keeping the little ones' minds working makes the time go by faster and the trip more enjoyable for all.

Always nurse or feed a baby a bottle on takeoff and landing. It helps the baby's ears adjust to the change in air pressure. If a toddler (or an adult for that matter) has a problem with ears, ask the flight attendant for a cup with a steaming hot, damp cloth in the bottom. Put the cup over the ear and the heat will help relieve the air pressure. We have done this many times. Babies with tubes in their ears never have problems with their ears while flying.

Having traveled millions of miles with my children at different ages and stages—by rail, auto, ship and plane I can tell you, it takes strength! **Make traveling easier by assembling a flight bag for each child that contains a few new toys or games and old favorites, as well as a few treats.** The bags should be small enough for the children to carry by themselves. If they travel frequently, children will quickly learn that what they take in their flight bag is very important for long flights or waiting time.

*D*on't hesitate to travel with children. As an army family, we had the opportunity to live in Europe for seven years. We traveled everywhere we could and I loved every second of it. **Traveling was great for our children, who were able to see that people are really the same everywhere.**

Some traditions from our childhood become so much a part of our lives that we continue them with our own families. After a long day out or coming home from a vacation, my mother would always say, "Home again, home again, jiggety-jig." Now we say the same thing, but add "That's what Grandma used to say." It never fails to bring a smile to us all.

Dr. Rich says:

Between eighteen months and two years old, it is permissible to put the child on the potty, perhaps before a nap or after a meal, but for no longer than thirty seconds. If you make them sit there until they go, they will get frustrated and you have prolonged the process for another six months. Don't make them hate the potty.

Bed wetting in an older child is a very delicate problem. A plethora of expensive products on the market profess to cure the habit, but I have seen no success with their bells and whistles. Bed wetting remains one of those mysteries that we only have theories about. Some of the possibilities are maturity of the plumbing and deepness of sleep, but no one knows for sure. I tell mothers who have children with this problem to treat them very sensitively and that the best thing they can do is get bigger laundry facilities.

Some toddlers want to be naked all of the time, some never want to take their clothes off—it's an individual thing. But use the correct terms, such as penis, vagina, breasts, etc., when talking to a toddler about his body. Up to ages four or five, if a child sees what the opposite sex looks like (even mother and father), they don't have the curiosity to go exploring.

Give traveling children Benadryl. Dose according to directions on package. Even though it is an antihistamine, it acts as a sedative. It will make them benign and happy.

CHILD CARE HINTS TO REMEMBER

I remember Mom saying

_____

_____

My own thoughts

_____

_____

CHAPTER NINE
Honey & Onions & Other Home Remedies

"How do you know when your child is sick? A sick child is languid and won't make eye contact. He'll have a hard time sleeping and eating, You can use down-to-earth information passed through the generations to comfort him at home, but if he has a high fever, take him to the doctor."
—Homer Rich, M.D.

As we collected home remedies from numerous grandmothers, we noticed that two ingredients came up time and again—honey and onions. The aroma of honey and onions conjures up memories of my own grandmother, making cough syrup on the big range in her kitchen. If Grandma believed a teaspoonful would stop a cough, I knew it must be so. Honey and onions are two of the world's most basic and ancient foods. The humble onion has been cultivated for millennia as a vegetable, yet it is one of the best natural medicines nature provides. Honey has also been around since prehistoric times and is used medicinally around the world. Both honey and onions are natural antibiotics that attack the bacteria that cause infections, and both are known for their anti-inflammatory and antiseptic qualities. Onions are highly nutritious, promote a healthier immune system, and are rich in vitamins and minerals. Honey is loaded with antioxidants, is also vitamin rich, and is good for the skin.

In this book, we have included just a sampling of the hundreds of uses for honey and onions. The following are recipes for this simple remedy, along with other home treatments from grandmothers around the world. Dr. Rich adds a pediatrician's view to round out your approach to home health.

Honey & Onions for Cough, Cold & More

Honey as a Natural Moisturizer: Unsupplemented wildflower honey has soothing effects on raw tissue and can be rubbed on surgical incisions, burns, and infected wounds. Thicken honey with cornstarch and cover the affected area with a sterile bandage after application.

Honey and Onion Cough Syrup: Quarter and slice one large onion. Place in a shallow dish and drizzle with enough honey to cover the onion. Let mixture steep in a warming oven until a thick syrup develops. For a cough, use one teaspoonful.

Honey and Onion Cough Syrup II: Add two tablespoons of diced onion to one half-cup of honey and cook over a double boiler for a few hours. Strain through a coffee filter before using.

Honey and Lemon Cough Syrup: Slowly toast a large lemon until it splits open. Add up to one-half teaspoon of honey to the juice from the lemon. Administer at hourly intervals until the cough is under control.

Honey, Onion, and Lemon Cough Syrup: Mix equal parts honey, fresh onion juice from shredded onion, and fresh lemon juice.

Mexican Cough Syrup: Chop onions fine, sprinkle with sugar, and let set until syrup forms.

Italian Milk-and-Honey Cough Elixir: Stir two tablespoons of honey into a cup of warm milk and drink three or four times a day.

Hot Toddy: Combine one teaspoon each of whiskey, honey, and water to ease cold symptoms.

Hot Toddy II: Combine one teaspoon each of brandy, lemon juice, and water to ease cold symptoms.

Onion Infusion: Pour one pint of boiling water over four medium-sized onions and let steep for two to three hours. Use to treat congestion, coughs, and bronchitis.

Onions as an Antiseptic: Traditionally, onions have been used to stave off a variety of infections. Rub the juice on a bite, scratch, or cut as an antiseptic.

Onion Breathing Aid: Cook an onion and breathe in the steam. Onion steam helps relieve sinus congestion.

Onion Breathing Aid II: Cut one large onion into six sections. Place onion pieces into a paper bag and breathe from the bag for ten seconds.

Vietnamese Cough Syrup: Steam kumquats and sugarcane to create a syrup.

Native American Sage Bath: Float several stalks of sage in a porous bag in a tub of warm water to ease a fever.

Native American Sage Tea: Boil approximately one tablespoon of sage leaves with a cup of water. Cover and steep for about ten minutes. Drink one half cup no more than three times throughout the day. Lemon juice and honey can be added for flavor. Pregnant or breast-feeding women should avoid sage.

Native American Sage Stick: Break a bunch of sage from the plant and hold it under the nose to stop it from running.

Austrian Sage Remedy: Gargle with sage tea or chew sage leaves for a sore throat.

Balsam: Use balsam as you would sage to facilitate breathing.

Eucalyptus Steam: Along with the antibiotic or antihistamine your doctor has prescribed, eucalyptus steam is especially soothing.

Eucalyptus Ointment: Rub a bandanna with eucalyptus ointment, then roll it up and tie it loosely around the neck.

Pineapple Juice: Fresh pineapple juice is good for congestion. It has more vitamin C, is less allergenic, and is easier on the stomach than citrus fruits. Pineapple juice breaks down the mucus to allow easier breathing.

Mexican Drink for Cold Prevention: Combine one-third cup apple cider vinegar and one teaspoon baking soda with one eight- to ten-ounce glass of water. Sweeten with sugar to taste. In the winter, our Mexican grandparents gave us this drink to prevent colds. I don't know how it worked, but we didn't get sick!

Ginger Tea: One of the best home remedies for colds is ginger. Ginger does a wonderful job cleaning out the bronchial tubes and sinus cavities and relieving congestion. Try it in tea form: to one cup of hot water, add just under one-half teaspoon each of ginger powder, fennel seeds, and cinnamon. Add a pinch of cloves, then let the herbs steep for about ten minutes. Strain the herbs out of the tea before drinking.

Lemon Tea: Squeeze the juice from a fresh lemon into a cup of boiling water and add two teaspoons honey for taste. Sip while warm.

Steam Tent: Build a makeshift tent over the child's bed using bed sheets, and use a steaming tea kettle to provide moist steam. However, never leave child's side when this method is used.

Mentholated Salve: I remember my mother rubbing a mixture of dry mustard and Vicks on my neck and then covering it with a special wool wrap. These wraps made me feel so sick, I wanted to get better! Today, mother's are cautioned not to use dry mustard or other materials that might burn the skin, but Vicks is still a good option.

Cold Air: When baby is excessively congested, wrap the baby in a nice warm blanket with only his little face exposed, and take him out into the cold night air. Cold air will help open up the lungs, reduce chest congestion and cough, and ease the wheezing.

Hot Baths and Hydration: Taking hot baths eases body aches, promotes healthy circulation, and hydrates the body. The best way to hydrate the body, of course, is to drink plenty of water. The body becomes dehydrated with the cold and flu as it loses fluids through sweating, diarrhea, and vomiting. Besides water—which children should sip regularly, even if they are not thirsty—offer vitamin-rich beverages such as fruit and vegetable juices and soup. Apple and dark grape juices are ideal, since they have properties that work against congestion and runny nose.

Mustard Bath: Stir small amounts of dry mustard into a very warm bath to relieve symptoms of pneumonia. After bathing, dry and wrap in a blanket.

Routines to Prevent the Spread of Germs: My mother, a meticulous woman of Hawaiian-Chinese descent, said, "Prevention is the best defense against illness." To this end, she color-coded many of our childhood items—one color for each child—believing this would increase sanitation and prevent the spread of germs. Every night and morning, she prepared a mixture of Hawaiian salt and hot water in our color-coded cups for each of us to gargle. She was absolutely convinced that we wouldn't get sick if we held strictly to this routine.

Gun Powder and Other Nonsense to Avoid: And who could forget diphtheria? No one who's ever suffered from it. This disease produces a toxin that causes inflammation of the heart and nervous system. Folks from the Old West were known to put a pinch of black gun powder on the back of the tongue each day for several days to remedy diphtheria. Gun powder seemed to work for this contagious disease when everything else failed. Of course, you wouldn't give a baby or anyone else gun powder now. In fact, we did a lot of things we know better than to do now. We used hydrogen peroxide, iodine, rubbing alcohol, and mercurochrome on cuts and scrapes, but now doctors say that's dangerous. We also spread butter on burns, but now we know it hurts more than it helps. In fact, we made plasters with goose grease mixed with turpentine, thinking it'd do a body good, which is just plain crazy. We also used syrup of Ipecac for accidental poisoning and tourniquets to stop bleeding. These are all outdated and considered dangerous today.

Dr. Rich says:

When a cough becomes the croup, it is a different story. First of all, you must get real scared—it is potentially a very serious thing. Ninety-five percent of the croup is viral or spasmodic croup. Take the baby out in the cool, fresh air or get into the shower with the baby and let him breathe the hot-water vapor. A vaporizer or cool steam may also be used. The other type of croup is tracheobronchitis. This type of croup is accompanied by fever and rapid respiratory rate. If the respiratory rate gets up to 55 breaths per minute (20 is normal) or the heart rate exceeds 150 beats per minute, then this is potentially very serious. Call your doctor or take the baby to the hospital. The first type of croup can last two or three nights; the second type lasts several days.

The brain regulates fever. Fever is a mechanism Mother Nature uses to combat infection, and it can be very worthwhile for a sick child, to a point. I like a sick child to demonstrate an elevated temperature to start with, because certain germs like strep and staph, as well as some viruses, cannot survive at a 104-degree temperature. Don't give the child Tylenol until the temperature gets over 102.5 degrees. Sweating will also help relieve a baby's fever. Here's a quick temperature formula: A child's pulse rate will increase ten beats per minute for each degree of fever.

Eighty percent of all respiratory infections in children are caused by viruses. When a child comes in with a runny nose, red throat, and low-grade fever, chances are it's a virus. If a child is eating well and the fever is low-grade and the symptoms are moderate, I give them an over-the-counter decongestant. Mothers can give symptomatic management with over-the-counter drugs. Antibiotics will work only if there is a bacterial infection.

Colic & Diarrhea

Burping: Whether you breast-feed or bottle-feed, you need to help your baby get rid of the huge amounts of air she is taking in. Burping is vital. Burp during feeding sessions, alternating between feeding and burping until you determine that the baby is full and comfortable. After feeding and burping, lay the baby on her left side. This helps the little bubbles come up easily.

Burping Faceup: In this variation on the tried-and-true, back-patting method of relieving stomach gas, the baby is held faceup. Sit with your elbows resting on your legs and hold your baby faceup with one hand, making sure the head remains higher than the stomach. With the other hand, gently pat the baby's back in an upward motion. Be patient and thorough with this maneuver—it will work.

Peppermint and Chamomile: These are two traditional herbal remedies that pediatricians still recommend for upset stomachs. Both work gently to soothe an upset stomach, stop stomach spasms, and reduce gas. My father told me my grandmother walked along the ditch bank to gather wild peppermint leaves, sometimes taking the older children to help her. She needed a large supply on hand for making peppermint tea, which she used for upset tummies and stomach gas. If you're nursing, drink lots and lots of peppermint tea. It will pass on to the baby and reduce colic. Older children can suck on a sugar cube with a drop of peppermint oil on it whenever they feel a bit queasy.

Dried Blueberries: Chew dried blueberries to prevent diarrhea as the Austrians did.

Massage: Relaxation helps a baby cope with colic and release gas. Rubbing the heels of a baby's feet helps relax his little body; so does tickling the arms and stroking the forehead.

Bland Diet for Nursing Mothers: To reduce colic, nursing mothers should stick to a simple and bland diet—avoid meats, home-canned foods, beans, and hot, spicy dishes.

Sedatives: Not for baby—for you! I had so much anxiety over my baby's colic that I resorted to getting a prescription sedative for myself to help me cope. The colic didn't seem as though it would ever end!

Dr. Rich says:

It is called the three-month colic, and guess how long it lasts? Three months! Colic is classic from six to ten o'clock at night—that is when babies scream. Why? We don't know. First, if the baby is on formula, I change to a soy-based formula. There are also antispasmodic drugs for difficult cases. Some babies have what's known as acid-reflux disease, and they are very miserable. They have trouble eating, they are in constant pain, and nothing seems to calm them down. Their lower esophagus is poorly developed, which allows the acidic gastric juices to leak from the stomach. When the baby gets full, it burps up the acid into the esophagus. Today, there are drugs to help babies with this problem, and they usually outgrow it.

Diarrhea is the bane of all pediatricians and mothers. Ninety-five percent of all cases of gastroenteritis (inflammation of the stomach and intestines) are caused by the rotavirus. Typhoid, paratyphoid, and salmonella cause another two to three percent. Gastroenteritis will last ten days no matter what you do. Years ago, we recommended a diet of tea, rice water, and boiled skim milk. Then a study was done in Philadelphia with twenty cases of intestinal flu. Half the children were put on a diet of tea, rice water, and boiled skim milk. The other half were put on a full nutritious diet. Both groups got well in ten days. The kids on the full diet had more stool, but the symptoms left in ten days. The kids on the diet of tea, rice water, boiled milk screamed and hollered for ten days because they were hungry, and then they got well. The researchers concluded that a restricted diet isn't necessary. Give the baby some Kaopektate or Donnagel to help relieve some of the symptoms, and don't become discouraged. If the baby is also vomiting or has a high fever, call the doctor right away.

Diaper Rash, Skin Irritations & Burns

Ben's Butt Paste for Diaper Rash: You can buy the ingredients for this ointment from a pharmacist: Burrows Solution, sterile water, Aquaphor, and zincoxide paste. First, mix an ounce of Burrows Solution with a cup of sterile water to create a modified Burrows Solution. Next, using a large mixer, thoroughly blend 300 grams of Aquaphor, 450 grams of zinc-oxide paste, and 150 milliliters of the modified Burrows Solution. Store tightly covered.

Cornstarch Diaper-rash Ointment: The best diaper rash treatment I ever used was a homemade mixture of Vaseline and cornstarch. This makes a thick paste.

Heavy-duty Moisture Barrier: The worst diaper rash I ever saw was on my baby grandson, who had acid-reflux disease, a severe type of colic. The instant a bowel movement touched his little bottom, his skin would erupt into a rash of painful lesions. Taking care of a baby with acid-reflux disease requires almost constant care. The acidic nature of their gastrointestinal systems causes all manner of problems, and they usually cry in misery most of the time. Severe cases of diaper rash require a preventative, heavy-duty moisture barrier like the ones used in hospitals. They can be purchased at a pharmacy or you can make one at home.

Soda Bath: Pour about one-half box of baking soda into warm bath water. Baking soda helps diaper rash sores dry up and heal faster.

Talc: In the 1940's, all we could find for diaper rash in my small, Italian village was a substance similar to clay that was sold by the pharmacy. The talc came as a solid block that we had to reduce to powder before we could sprinkle it on our baby's bottom. Strange as it sounds, the talc worked like magic on the diaper rash.

Airing Out: Prevention is the best defense against diaper rash. Remember, airing out your baby's bottom for just five minutes a day helps avoid diaper rash.

Oatmeal Bath: In a food processor or blender, process one cup of oatmeal until powdery. Pour it into the foot of an old nylon and tightly tie it up. Place the sock in a bath of warm water to soothe diaper rash and other skin irritations.

Dr. Rich says:

Two things cause the majority of diaper rashes: (1) inadequate diaper changing and, (2) most commonly, yeast infection. Yeast infections originate from an overgrowth of yeast in the bowels, and they require both a medicine by mouth and a special ointment such as Mycolog-ll Cream or Nystatin. Our intestinal tracts are full of germs. So, as a precaution, I recommend a protective layer of a good ointment on the baby's bottom to create a barrier against the irritation of bowel movements and urine. Some children may be more susceptible to diaper rash because they have very sensitive skin or because of harsh washing detergents.

Sour Milk for Sunburns: Grandmothers on the farm treated sunburns with sour milk. The fat content of milk is soothing, so make a compress or just smear it on for sunburn pain. Be sure to wash off the milk to avoid having your skin smell sour.

Eggshells: To eliminate boils, use the skin from the inside of an eggshell. While the skin is still damp and sticky, lay it over the boil and let it dry.

Burn Remedies: Apply a fluoride toothpaste to burns to lessen the reddening, pain, and itching. Apply a paste of baking soda and water to blistering skin. Soak gauze in ice-cold milk and apply to burned area for three minutes.

Teething

Today's Tips for Teething: Just when you think your newborn is finally ready to sleep through the night, teething begins. The problem is that many mothers don't recognize the crying for what it is until the first little tooth pops out. When a baby's gums become red and swollen, try these suggestions:

- Rub the gums with your finger.
- Offer your baby clean, hard, cold surfaces to chew on, like frozen teething rings.
- Give the baby a cold washcloth to suck on.
- Give an older baby teething biscuits, crusty bread, or peeled apple wedges.
- Rub the gums with oil of cloves, Anbesol, or Numzit.

Yesteryear's Tip for Teething: I remember my grandmother rubbing whiskey on sore gums.

Dr. Rich says:

Mothers should not panic when their baby suffers teething pain. Teething causes teeth, and nothing more. Some mothers don't realize their baby has a tooth until they hear it click on the spoon. Other babies scream for two weeks before a tooth comes in. The difference lies in their threshold for pain. The average baby gets its first tooth between six and seven months old. However, some babies are born with two teeth and some don't get their first tooth until they are fourteen months old. Teething is a process, and a baby is teething long before the tooth actually erupts. You can buy a number of things at the store to rub on the gums, which is very good for the pharmaceutical manufacturers, but they don't do anything for the teeth. I recommend a dose of Tylenol every four hours.

Earaches

Onions for Earaches: The onion, a natural antibiotic, can alleviate the pain of an earache. Bake an onion wrapped in foil until tender. Then squeeze the onion through gauze to extract the juice. Draw warm onion juice into a medicine dropper and insert a drop or two into the sore ear, then place a small wad of cotton over it. This method is particularly useful for infants and helps them sleep better. You'll be amazed at how quickly the infection clears up.

Onions for Earaches II: Bake an onion until just tender and cut it in half. Wrap half the onion in gauze and carefully bandage the onion over the ear with a strip of stretchy fabric or tape. Make sure the onion is not too hot! The warmth of the onion is comforting, and the onion's natural oils are absorbed into the bloodstream, which speeds up recovery.

Dr. Rich says:

Cold air does not cause ear infections. Ear infections are caused by an infection in the throat that goes up the eustachian tubes and infects the ears. Cold air can interfere with blood circulation to the brain, which in turn alters the fever mechanism; the chilling that results can give rise to infection, since you always have germs in your system. But fresh air does not cause ear infections; neither does wind.

Insect Bites

Meat Tenderizer: An old remedy for bites and stings is meat tenderizer. Make a thick paste of water and powdered meat tenderizer and apply it directly on the insect bite or sting. It breaks down the venom and takes the sting out!

Raw Onion: Rub a cut onion on a bug bite or bee sting.

Bruises & Muscular Pain

Alpine Flower: Make a tincture of the alpine flower, Arnica Montana, and rub onto bruises several times a day.

Relief for Growing Pains: Before going to bed, tie a handkerchief snuggly around the leg at the calf for leg aches and growing pains.

Plasters: One treatment that is often remembered fondly is the plaster. A plaster was made with dry mustard or other spices such as nutmeg or cloves. The skin of the chest was prepared with Watkins Petro-Carbo Salve from the drugstore or with lard. A piece of flour sack (cheesecloth) was placed on top of the ointment, which was then sprinkled with the spice. The whole preparation was then covered to produce maximum warmth and watched very closely for the skin to turn pink. Although widely accepted in the years before modern medicines, they are now considered very dangerous. Dr. Rich says the risk of a painful burn is much too great to consider using a plaster in this day and age.

Plasters II: To relieve a mother's arthritis pain, mix together two parts flour with one part dry mustard powder, then add water to make a paste. Spread it on a clean cloth, fold it in half, and press it against the skin. Don't put the mixture directly on the skin, since it can burn. You can also use this to loosen phlegm or relieve sore muscles. Again, Dr. Rich says plasters risk painful burns and should not be used on children. Use on yourself with extreme caution.

Vietnamese Coining: For body aches and pains, rub the area of discomfort with the edge of a warm coin. The skin may become slightly irritated from this treatment.

Grandma's Old-Fashioned Remedies

The Dropper: Administering medicine to a baby can be very frustrating. The best way to dispense the medicine is from a medicine dropper placed under the baby's tongue. Otherwise, the baby might spit the medicine out.

Sugar Tits: For a pacifier, wrap a sugar cube in a small square of fabric and tie it shut with thread.

Honey-Baked Onions to Prevent or Remedy Illness: Eating onions regularly can prevent and remedy illness. Peel and halve six yellow onions. Place cut side up in microwave pan. Dribble with honey and dot with butter. Add a little water to the pan and cover with plastic. Microwave on high for eight to ten minutes. Rotate one-quarter turn after three minutes and repeat again in three minutes.

Austrian Herbal Remedies: In Austria, we gathered flowers, berries, and herbs to use as medicines. Administering the remedies was the easy part. The difficult part was collecting them in the woods and alpine meadows, then drying and storing them for later use. For centuries, most medicines were herbs; the tradition of herbal remedies held strong through the 18th century and is still valuable today.

Dr. Rich says:

I consider myself a dinosaur, since I attended medical school in the 1940's and have practiced for over fifty years. My staff and I worked up some numbers—figuring I have seen on the average of twenty-five patients a day, five days a week, fifty weeks a year, for fifty years, I have had over 300,000 office calls. I have learned some things! I always took calls from my moms as well—sometimes as many as a hundred a day. I knew at the other end of that call was a very worried mother. The mothers in my office did not resent the time I spent on the phone because they knew I would do the same for them. With medical advice, lots of love, and good common sense, moms and dads can enjoy healthy, happy, contented babies.

Well-Baby Visits

A well-baby visit is a periodic visit for six months to make sure the baby is growing and developing normally, to answer questions that the mother may have, and to immunize. I asked my mothers to check in for monthly visits.

The Six-Foot Imaginary Circle

Babies are very susceptible to infections for the first month. Draw a six-foot imaginary circle around the baby and try to keep family and friends away for a month. By then, he has a better chance and a little more resistance. After about one month, babies need to start getting exposed to germs to build up the immune system.

Vaccine Schedule

- *Hepatitis A at two years with a booster six to eighteen months later*

- *Hepatitis B at birth, one month, and six to nine months*

- *Polio at two, four, and six months and at four to six years*

- *DPT (diphtheria, pertussis or whooping cough, tetanus) at two, four, six, and twelve to fifteen months and at four to six years*

- *HIB (H influenza, type B) at two, four, and six months and a booster at fifteen months*

- *MMR (measles, mumps, rubella) at fifteen months and four to six years*

- *VAR (varicella or chicken pox) at twelve months*

Growth Predictor

A baby doubles its birth weight at five months, triples at a year, and quadruples at age two. Think of a five-month-old baby weighing fifteen pounds—that baby is drinking a quart of milk a day. That is why babies gain so rapidly, because they take in such huge amounts of calories in relation to their body weight.

Height Prediction Formula

A child at one year of age has reached approximately twenty-five percent of his or her adult height. If a child is twenty-nine and one-half inches tall at age one, he or she should probably be about five feet, eleven inches as an adult.

CHILD CARE HINTS TO REMEMBER

I remember mom saying

_____

_____

My own thoughts

_____

_____

ACKNOWLEDGMENTS

Thank you Heidi Massey for your inspiration and Jo Packham for making it happen!

CONTRIBUTING GRANDMOTHERS

We are also grateful for the dear grandmothers who shared their priceless stories and advice with us. Below are the names and ages of the women who contributed to this book, as well as a line or two of what they had to say about themselves.

Elsie Clark Ray Adams
8 grandchildren, 13 great-grandchildren; born Lander, Wyoming, in a log cabin

Elaine Reiser Alder
12 grandchildren, freelance writer

Cleo Remington Atkin
8 grandchildren, 2 great-grandchildren; political activist

Judy Schiffman Bangerter
10 grandchildren; professional fundraiser and political activist

Donna Rae Barlow
4 grandchildren, mother of twins

Helen Bateman
16 grandchildren, 2 great-grandchildren; Family Life teacher

Carol Ann Petersen Cook, 71
6 grandchildren

Buehla Dixon Coublouq
4 grandchildren, 1 great-grandchild; California

Fern Bagnall Davis
9 grandchildren, 7 great-grandchildren

Filomena De Simone
10 grandchildren, 6 great-grandchildren; born Southern Italy

Fredonna Strickler Dixon
8 grandchildren, 15 great-grandchildren; elementary-school teacher, singer

Ernestine Esquivel
3 grandchildren; Santa Fe, New Mexico

Vaudis Day Evans
6 grandchildren, 6 great-grandchildren; the "cookie grandma," loves to tap dance

Olga Figgs
1 grandchild,1 great-grandchild; Vineland, New Jersey

Myrle Dixon Fowler
17 grandchildren, 30 great-grandchildren, 21 great-great-grandchildren

Beth Foxley
14 grandchildren, 16 great-grandchildren; fun and lively spirit

Anne Stevenson Freimuth
7 grandchildren, Irish-immigrant grandparents

Michaelene Grassle
10 grandchildren; author, speaker, former Primary general president

Sandy Grim
15 grandchildren; Miss Roy 1962, dedicated mother and grandmother

JoAnn H. Hamilton
Combined family of 21 children, author, motivational speaker

Jeannette Havas
7 grandchildren, 11 great-grandchildren; Holocaust survivor

Sandy Havas
14 grandchildren; art center director

Ardeth L. Howser
12 grandchildren of multicultural ancestry, Kailua, Hawaii, landscaper

Wanda Dixon Hunt
12 grandchildren, 13 great-grandchildren; mother of a professional baseball player

Norma H. Inouye
7 grandchildren, 4 great-grandchildren; grocery store owner

Valerie J. Kelson
13 grandchildren, including a set of triplets

Sharon King
9 grandchildren; the "reading grandma," teacher, and literacy specialist

Dorothy Lai
8 grandchildren; Orange, California; great influence on her family

Carolyn Levitt
2 grandchildren; Pediatrician, St. Paul, Minnesota

Judy Lind
1 grandchild; Honolulu, Hawaii; dedicated to helping abused children

Telitha Lindquist
29 grandchildren; Ogden, Utah; community advocate

Sue Cramblet Massey
7 grandchildren; active in church and community

Joan Maw
19 grandchildren; homemaker and golfer

Margie P. Mayfield
6 grandchildren; Ooltewah, Tennessee; business owner

Mae Mecham
13 grandchildren; the "burrito grandma," calligraphy expert

Linda Miller
3 grandchildren; child and health advocate

Vada Nielsen
21 grandchildren, 17 great-grandchildren

Flora Ogan
5 grandchildren; Ogden, Utah; retired newspaper editor

Suzanne Osmond
8 sons, 6 grandchildren; Orem, Utah; musical family

Thien Pham
2 grandchildren; Kien Giang, Viet Nam

Janiel Paris
2 grandchildren; Las Vegas, Nevada; social worker

Irene Drake Parker
25 grandchildren, 20 great-grandchildren; teacher, Homecoming Royalty 2004

Grethe B. Peterson
12 grandchildren; kind and generous heart

Kathleen S. Peterson
27 grandchildren

Evangeline V. Ross
3 grandchildren; Inglewood, California

Velma Saunders
2 grandchildren, born in Louisiana, great-grandmother was a slave

Katherine Dixon Schofield
12 grandchildren, 16 great-grandchildren; youngest of 14 children

Margaret Seklemian
2 grandchildren; Denver, Colorado

Lou Shurtliff
5 grandchildren; teacher, state representative, mahjong player

Catherine Singletary
*4 grandchildren; Rancho Santa Margarita, California;
retired social worker*

Barbara B. Smith
*39 grandchildren, 34 great-grandchildren; author,
former Relief Society General President*

Johanna (Mutti) Smola
2 grandchildren; Villach, Austria

Sally Fowler Steglich
5 grandchildren; family historian

Eleda Vee Stokes
16 grandchildren, 5 great-grandchildren; songwriter and poet

Dee Meyer Street
3 grandchildren; mom of an Olympic athlete

Ruth Sugimoto
5 grandchildren, 5 great-grandchildren, onion farm owner

Ann Swensen Sumner
7 grandchildren; speech and hearing therapist

Jane A. Thompson
6 grandchildren; special-education teacher

Carolyn L. Thompson
17 grandchildren; amateur actress

Phyllis Tsosie
19 grandchildren, 2 great-grandchildren; born on the Navajo reservation, makes jewelry and weaves rugs

Carmen L. Vigil
23 grandchildren, 37 great-grandchildren; Tucumcari, New Mexico; business owner

Ekase Zenovia Ward
Guardian angel to her descendants

Shauna Swensen Weight
11 grandchildren; storyteller and amateur actress

Terry Willis
2 grandchildren, artist and children's advocate

Debra Wood
1 grandchild; victim-services coordinator

EDITORIAL CONTRIBUTORS

The contributors and their families are long-time friends and partners in a wide variety of projects. Along with professional careers in education, marketing, and advocacy they have been involved in a wide variety of civic pursuits including numerous local, state, and national boards. They also have many years of Junior League participation and training and have extensive volunteer experience. Now mostly retired, they enjoy spending time with their husbands, eight children, eight spouses-in-law, 24 grandchildren, as well as other family members and friends. They are excited to introduce *From Grandma to You* to a new generation.

"Grandmas hold our tiny hands for just a little while but our hearts forever."

Author Unknown

In Memory of Dr. Homer R. Rich

Since *From Grandma to You* was originally published, our dear friend and collaborator, Dr. Rich, has passed away. He was ninety-one years old. We have missed his wit, wisdom, and enthusiasm for our book and know he would be pleased and proud that we are re-releasing it to another generation of new mothers. Dr. Rich cared for all children: during the night and on holidays, in the office or at home, when the weather was bad or he was tired, or whether they could pay or not. Hundreds of little patients and mothers appreciate and love him for the influence he was in their lives. He was an example of dedication, care and concern to everyone he associated with (the three of us included). He was loved by all and we feel grateful and proud to continue his legacy in our book, *From Grandma to You*.